Living Room
makeovers

Salli Brand

D1396652

B

BETTERWAY BOOKS
CINCINNATI, OHIO

Contents

Take a look at the colors you can see around you. Now, for a few moments, imagine a world without color. It's not easy. We use color automatically in our lives for pleasure, business, and guidance. Road signs use color to give us information or warn us of danger. Traffic lights tell us to stop or continue by using red, green, and yellow. Imagine the difficulties a world without color would pose to corporations bent on building at-a-glance identities, or to safety organizations, which rely on instant recognition.

The extreme of this use of color has to be advertising placards that no longer even mention the brand or product being sold to us. Yet the message is still clearly understood because of color association.

You will instinctively choose certain colors when buying clothes. Why? You will know that a particular color suits you, or maybe you are more comfortable in another. Perhaps the yellow of your shirt makes you stand out from the crowd. Color in the home can have exactly the same associations as the clothing you wear; it can relax or revitalize, warm you up or cool you down. It can even be anonymous, making way for your accessories and furnishings. The incredible transformation qualities of color are infinite, and the choice is yours.

Although today's demand for color has led to a huge growth in paint colors available, it can be daunting knowing how to achieve the desired effect in the home or where to start when combining colors. Professional

interior designers use their knowledge and experience to make color and decorating choices that will work on a practical level as well as aesthetically. It is this type of advice and information that is included here.

By concentrating on a single room, each title in the Makeover Series takes into account the very different color and paint considerations each room demands. This is very much in tune with the way interior decoration is approached, concentrating on the overall color choices for one room at a time.

This book should be used as a practical guide to selecting paints and colors for your living room, creating the desired environment. Discussion on color theory will enable you to follow the same processes as the professionals when choosing and using color in the home. Practical advice on paint products and their suitability is combined with inspirational examples showing the use of color in a room. This knowledge will allow you to manipulate your own space.

A room can look radically different when the colors and paint finishes are changed. This is illustrated here by the different makeovers of an identical room. The same room was painted and accessorized six times. In these makeovers color is used in many different ways—as paint and on furnishings and accessories—creating an all-over look. The individual projects allow as little or as much of that look to be re-created or adapted to suit other decorative schemes.

Each makeover includes basic information on initial preparation and techniques, as well as advice on how to complete the different projects. By "basic," we mean "from the beginning," thereby allowing an absolute beginner in the field of home decoration to get a handle on putting ideas into practice. Everything you need to know to get started is contained within these projects.

All of the projects featured were completed within two days. If you allow four days, you will be able to work at a relaxed pace and enjoy yourself as well.

Using color in your living room

Paint and color in the home are only surface decorations, but they play an important role. Just as clothes, cosmetics, and perfumes offer a snapshot of a personality to the onlooker, so the decorating schemes in homes and the atmosphere produced offer much the same. For example, the living room is usually more inviting than the study in the same house. It will, after all, be responsible for creating an atmosphere for the entire house.

COLOR AND MOOD

Color is believed to have an important psychological impact on mood, well-being, energy, and motivation. Autumnal colors are considered to be relaxing and thus not suitable for offices, whereas peppermint greens are supposed to encourage alertness. It follows, therefore, that restaurants and bars favor warm autumnal shades, to relax the clientele and make them stay longer, while the gym at a leisure center is sure to be painted in a fresh pale tone to keep people awake, training hard, and going back time and again! In the 1980s, some corporate environments even employed bright garish colors in the restrooms in the

The wall color in a room is the major influence on the overall atmosphere. The cool blue room (top left) has gone all the way with blue walls, woodwork, and accessories, adding just a splash of brightening yellow in the curtains. The yellow room (bottom left) makes use of a jamboree of New England muted tones for the woodwork and accessories and yet still sings warm yellow.

7

MIXING COLORS

In today's world of color, the rules are continually being broken and experimentation is the key. In past years one would have heard a sharp intake of breath if colors such as orange and pink were used together. Now it may be considered daring but that is all. It is not against the rules; colors in your living room can be mixed and matched at will.

The color wheel featured on page 29 offers a quick and easy way of combining colors for more timid designers. In fact, we are all familiar with the basic combinations and probably use them instinctively as colors that "go" together. Black and white, for example, are opposites and an obvious choice where contrast is essential, such as on the printed page. If you take black and white down a little you will find navy blue and cream: colors that are quite simply stunning for home decor. A little further down will take you to tones of beige or yellow against reddish purples such as burgundy, which can be softer on the eye. If you are uncertain, the color wheel holds its own as a great adviser.

hope that the colors would be daunting and discourage long conversations between members of staff behind the scenes, and in this way minimize time spent away from the actual workplace not making money.

Pattern, too, is used in some commercial environments to control actions. One of the major clothing chains in the United Kingdom laid carpets with a herringbone zigzag pattern, running from the main doors into the store, in all of their large stores. This use of a subconscious guiding line encouraged customers to walk further into the store and thus see more of the merchandise on sale. It is quite probable that much more money was spent in the stores as a direct result of this manipulation by color and pattern.

CHOOSING COLORS

The colors selected will be the primary factor in creating a mood or atmosphere. The living room is a tricky room to paint because, in most homes, it is a room that is used both during the day and in the evening. It may also serve different purposes at different times of the day. Maybe children play here, and perhaps it is used as a workspace during the day and a place to eat and relax in during the evening. In these dual-purpose living rooms the choice of color can be vital.

The blue room on page 80 was painted so that it could be used for children during the day and still be a comfortable evening environment for adults. Although perhaps not as charming as the evening warmth of the creams used in the room on page 68, it is nevertheless clean and functional for all times of the day. It would be difficult to imagine children playing in a magnolia-colored environment when they would be better stimulated by bright primary colors such as red and green. Likewise, it would be hard to relax in a primary-painted living room. The crisp pale blues used in this room are something of a compromise between the two requirements.

There are several factors to bear in mind when decorating and accessorizing your living room. First, consider how often the room is used and at what times of the day. If the living room is only used in the evening, any color from the entire spectrum can be used. You may safely choose warm colors, such

as terra-cottas and deep golds, and at the other end of the spectrum you may also select crisp clean whites and other accent colors. Second, you will need to consider lighting, and third, the purpose and size of the living room before you launch into decorating.

Take some time selecting the colors for your living room. Perhaps even paint some large boards in what you believe to be your chosen color. Prop these boards against the wall and live with them for a few days in a variety of light conditions before making a final decision.

EFFECT OF LIGHTING

Natural lighting can limit your color choice. If your living room receives very little natural light, care must be taken not to make

F U C H S I A

PINK

Using pink and purple creates a bold statement in your decor. Intense fuchsia pink works to great effect against blues such as ultramarine and delft blue. Try shiny mirrors on a fuchsia pink or purple wall—they add an amazing flash of light. While this choice of color reflects fashions and may date quickly, it can easily be changed if used in a small area.

the room look too somber. Autumnal colors such as deep burnt oranges and terra-cottas can have this effect. Blues in a shady room can look cold, and white can look too stark and clinical. If, however, your room receives a lot of light and sunshine then you may like to capitalize on this fact and create a sunny haven.

Normal off-the-shelf light bulbs have a yellowing effect. If you take a good look at a white room in the evening, you will really be looking at yellows rather than whites. It is not time to change your lighting; rather, consider it when choosing your colors. Most colors become warmer as yellow is added to them with evening lighting but beware of blues and purples, which will become greener or grayer respectively, while reds become more orange. For a continued natural sunlight effect you could try the daylight-simulation bulbs available from most stores, made from pale blue glass. Try only one to start with as you might find you prefer conventional evening lighting after all.

THE FUNCTIONAL CONSIDERATIONS

Before decorating your living room, consider its function. Does it serve as a dining room as well? If so, you might want to reflect this dual function in the color scheme. Perhaps your living room serves also as a playroom or nursery. If so, you will be aware that color is not quite as important as washability and ease of maintenance. It is possible to combine the two, however, if you select your paints carefully and choose fast-drying ones that you can touch up when required.

Keep a note of the exact name of the paint color you eventually select for your living room in order to be able to buy it again if you ever need to patch up areas of damage. Matching through guesswork is very difficult.

Also bear in mind that some paints are mildly toxic and should not be used in areas where children play. There has been a developing vogue for historical paints, manufactured to the original recipe and wearing a high price tag. Beware of these: muted greens used to be made with cyanide. While this is almost certainly not in today's mix, who knows what ingredient is used in its place?

If you are tinting your paints with tubes of artist's oils, check the health label on each tube, as toxicity could be an issue. Watch out for the words "cadmium" and "chromium" on the color names. Own-brand latex paints as a rule are nontoxic.

The more long-wearing paints, such as eggshell and gloss finish paints, will smell for a few days after application as the oils and thinners dry out. These more chemical-based paints will last

BLUE GREEN

AQUA

Aqua is now moving out of the bathroom and into other rooms in the home, and about time too. These pale tones can be even fresher than white and create an atmosphere of energy and cleanliness. Aqua also looks stunning against matte black, if you are brave enough to try it. Be aware that artificial light changes aqua to yellowish green.

A P P L E

GREEN

Good enough to eat and as vibrant a color as any in the spectrum, apple green often inhibits decorators with its sheer intensity. However, it is a good color in both daylight and evening light and works well with simple colors such as off-whites and purest white. Green also makes you feel hungry.

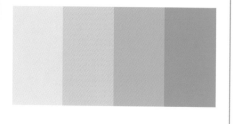

longer, with greater luster; it could be worth the aroma as the price for perfection. Keep a newly painted room well ventilated and, most importantly, dry for a while; this not only helps to eliminate chemical smells but will aid the drying and curing process and promise years of good service from your efforts.

ROOM SIZE AND COLOR

The size of the living room will also affect choice of color. Some colors "recede," which means that they add to a feeling of space, while some "advance," which can make a room look either smaller or cosier, depending on how you use them. Red and green are the most forceful examples of this; red advances and can make a room look smaller, while green recedes and can produce the opposite effect. Red against a green background advances so much that the effect is almost three-dimensional.

All the main makeover pictures in this book are of the same room. Although it looks completely different with the varying colors and tones, the dimensions of the room are the same. The cream room (see page 68) looks airy and spacious, while the brown room (see page 58) seems small and cosy. For an illustration of the most dramatic and surprising difference, put a finger in the book on the yellow room (see page 36) and on the pastel room (see page 26), and flick from one to the other a few times. You will see how the pastel room looks somehow longer and lower and the yellow room seems higher and wider.

The photographs were all taken at roughly the same time of day, so lighting conditions cannot be used as an excuse. Neither were the paints shaded or changed on the walls of the rooms, which means that exactly the same treatment was used across an entire wall. In the brown room (see page 58) the shadows beside the window (on the back wall) were rather cool and gray compared with the warmth of the rest of the room. If this area of shadow had affected the entire wall, a lighter tone would have been used on the back wall to compensate for the coolness. Just one or two shades lighter on a paint chart will make a difference without being too noticeable.

The pastel room (see page 26) looks long and narrow because the divisions between the various colors tell your brain to move along the walls or around the room. Thus your sense is of the width of the walls. In the yellow room (see page 36), with fewer divisions and a paint effect in the form of vertical stripes, your eyes are drawn up and down. A white ceiling is like a blank expanse of nothing to the brain, so you look right up the yellow walls and

BOOK ROOM

RED

This deep red creates a feeling of warmth and relaxation and works well with gold. This color is not for tiny rooms as red advances but it is perfect for library-type living rooms, as its name suggests. A relaxing color with less kick than crimson or scarlet, book room red often appeals to men.

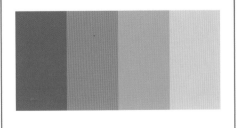

A flat mirror above the fireplace reflects terra-cottas from the opposite wall with an added brightness and creates the illusion of an alcove and more space.

S U N F L O W E R
YELLOW

Yellow is a color associated with cheerfulness. Deep yellows can be difficult to accessorize but work well with dark wood. Regal purple is the opposite color to this bright yellow; if these colors are used together they create a very rich atmosphere. Alternatively, use yellow with green for a garden feel. Look in a florist's window for inspirational ideas on how to mix yellow with other colors.

onward into nothing; thus the sense of height is stimulated. Bear in mind, however, that a white ceiling is not always the perfect finishing touch for a room as it can look unfinished.

D I V I D I N G C O L O R

The way in which you divide color will also alter the effect in a living room. Many horizontal breaks, such as different colors above and below a chair rail, or above and below a picture rail, will serve to draw the eye along the walls and thus give a feeling of a lower ceiling. On the other hand, painted stripes running vertically draw the eye up and create a feeling of height.

The color of the ceiling is important. The paler it is, the higher it will look. If you are aiming for a warm feel, consider a cream or pale tone of one of the colors featured elsewhere in the room. For example, a pinkish beige ceiling in a terra-cotta room will go almost unnoticed, whereas a white ceiling will provide a stark contrast and draw the eye upwards. However, take care with intensely colored ceilings as they can look rather amateurish: sunflower yellow on top of sky blue and pale yellow would not look very good.

C O M P R O M I S I N G

There may be a dilemma to overcome between what you want the room to look like and what will serve the room best. For example, you might want a bright white room with a polished wooden floor. But this would not be practical for a cosy living room where you watch television and entertain friends, and certainly not if you have children. The color choice needs to be practical rather than dictated by emotions; compromise is essential, as is your choice of paint type. Sometimes the cost of a shiny finish will be prohibitive compared with the cost of matte paints. There may also be times when the washability of the paint is essential and thus a shinier surface is worth the extra cost.

Intense colors, such as deep greens and terracottas, will always look superb in evening light, but consider how much they will be viewed in natural light. The effect can be completely different. It is advisable to try a test area first. Paint a large area going around a corner so that you can view it without seeing any of the original walls. Then look at it for several days in all light conditions before making a decision. Small patches of color will help you to know if you like the color but will not show you how the color will look in your room.

Colors can look different from the paint chip because of lighting and the effect of accessories and furniture. Shades of yellow in particular often cause a problem as they can look greenish.

N E U T R A L

NATURALS

Natural shades evoke a feeling of comfort in some people. The shades used in this photograph reduce the temperature and have a subtle outdoor feel to them. Rooms can be accessorized with items in other natural shades, such as baskets and dried grasses, or they work well with modern chrome. Naturals are as far as you can go toward autumnal shades without creating a cosy, warm air in a room.

Paint Products

The selection of paints, varnishes, and other products for decorating that are available can be confusing for an enthusiastic amateur. These pages will help you through the maze of products and guide you to the correct selection for the project you are undertaking and the surfaces on which you intend to apply it.

Paint is colored pigment suspended in a medium that makes it spreadable and gives it an acceptable drying time. Paint also contains the relevant chemicals to ensure that it does not rub off easily and that the color will not fade too much. It can be helpful to understand how paint is manufactured. There are two main processes involved: one for water-based paints and one for oil-based paints.

WATER-BASED PAINTS

Water-based paints are known as latex paints. They are water soluble and are made by pushing ground pigment (color in its purest form) into a solution of water and polyvinyl acetate (PVA) resin. PVA is a type of plastic. The pigment is forced into the resin and water at such high speed that it breaks up and disperses evenly. When you apply a PVA paint to your walls you are effectively applying a skin of colored plastic and water. The water evaporates and you are left with an even coating of colored plastic. The greater the shine on the PVA paint, the higher the ratio of plastic to water.

OIL-BASED PAINTS

Oil-based paints, such as eggshell and gloss, are more complicated to make and as a result are more expensive to buy. You can expect oil-based paints to last much longer than many water-based ones. Oil-based paint is made by first making a "binder," which is a mixture of linseed oil, acid, and alcohol. To this are added some thinners (mineral spirits) and ground white pigment, and this is then mixed. The pigment does not break up and disperse during this process so the mixture is then ground in a mill to ensure that an evenly whitened paint base results. Finally, more thinners are added, along with a chemical drier and some stainers. The product goes through a staining process before it is officially called paint. You may be familiar with paint base; this is the product to which home decorating stores add stainers in order to color the paint to your requirements. So, when you apply oil-based paint you are simply covering your surface with colored oils. As it contains all these chemicals, it smells strong.

PRIMER

Primer can be either water or oil based. It is used on bare wood to seal the surface and prevent the wood from swelling when the undercoat and top coat are applied.

UNDERCOAT

Undercoat can be either water or oil based. It is a thin surface preparation and is used to seal walls and woodwork before the top coat is applied. It has a matte finish.

LATEX FLAT PAINT

Latex flat paint is practical and inexpensive to use for covering large areas quickly. As it is water based, it does not have an offensive smell and has no shine at all. Flat paints are difficult to wash if they become dirty but can be touched up very quickly and easily.

LATEX SATIN PAINT

Latex satin paint is much the same as latex flat paint but easier to clean if it gets dirty and has a slight shine to it. For creating paint techniques your base coat must have a slight shine, so this type of paint is recommended in place of flat finishes. There are now some washable latex paints on the market that help to overcome the difficulties of keeping a flat-painted surface looking like new.

EGGSHELL PAINT

Oil-based or eggshell paint has a definite satin shine to it and usually a greater intensity and luster of color. It is more expensive than latex paint but will last at least twice as long. Eggshell paint has an offensive smell, and it is recommended that, when using it, you work in a well-ventilated area to prevent inhalation of the fumes. Eggshell paint takes longer to dry than water-based paints. However, the effect of oil-based paint on a surface is more professional than water-based paint.

GLOSS PAINT

Gloss paint is almost always oil based and has a full gleam to it. It is difficult to apply and should be brushed over a surface in two or three thin coats using a good-quality brush. Over time, the shine of the gloss will reduce and it will need repainting.

RADIATOR PAINT

Radiator paint has a lower quantity of ingredients that may yellow with heat. It also contains ingredients which keep the paint from peeling off a hot surface or softening when the radiators are on. Radiator paint is much more expensive to buy than other paints and the choice of colors is limited. If you are prepared to repaint your radiators as time goes by, then you can use any shade of eggshell paint. Always work on a cold surface.

TILE PRIMERS

Tile primers are designed for those who cannot afford the luxury of new tiles when changing the room decor. You can safely and effectively paint over your old tiles for a new look. Apply tile primer in two coats, leaving at least 16 hours between each coat as it dries very slowly. When the primer is dry, you can paint the tiles in any color you choose, using an eggshell paint for a long life.

UNIVERSAL STAINERS

These are colored stains in liquid form that can be added to water-based or oil paints to adjust the color. They are available in traditional artist's colors. Try raw umber for "dirtying" a color. Avoid black unless you are seeking a graying effect; it can be too artificial.

VARNISH

Varnish is just like paint but clear. Most varnish comes through the initial production stages as clear gloss. Silicon powders are added to make a satin or flat finish. Since these powders settle in the can, it is imperative to stir the varnish well before and regularly during use. Varnishes that claim to bring out the beauty of your wood may have some yellow colorants added to them. You can stain varnish very easily for your own use by stirring in some artist's colors. Use oil colors for polyurethane varnishes and acrylics for water-based varnishes.

Generally, the thinner the varnish, the easier it is to apply and the better will be the quality of your finished work. Before buying varnish, shake the cans and choose the ones in which the contents sound most like water. Very thick varnishes, such as yacht varnish, look good after only a couple of coats, but the coats are very difficult and time consuming to apply. It is preferable to apply four or five coats of a thinner varnish for a smooth finish.

WOOD STAIN

Wood stain is most often used for coloring untreated or bare wood. It can be either water or spirit based. Wood stain soaks deep into the grain of the wood but is transparent so that the original grain will still show through. Apply the wood stain in generous quantities and wipe the surface with a soft cloth when dry. Wood stain does not actually protect raw wood, and you must apply a coat of varnish or wax over the surface after coloring it for protection.

WAX

Wax offers an easy way to bring some protection and sheen to wood. Wax will nourish and protect most wooden surfaces and can be repaired and touched up easily. Beeswax is still one of the best wood polishes (and also smells very pleasant). All you need to do is apply the wax just like a floor polish, let it dry, and then buff with a soft cloth. Reapply wax on a surface from time to time as the sheen dulls.

Waxes containing colorants are also available; these will stain the wood as you go. You may need to carry out several applications of colored wax before you achieve the color shown on the can. For the initial treatment of wood with wax you may benefit from hiring a professional buffer, such as those used to polish cars.

GLAZE

Glaze is another medium that can be colored for use in creating special paint effects such as ragging and dragging. In simple terms it makes the color slippery and movable. The glaze is applied with a paintbrush or roller and then, while it is still wet, it is manipulated (see pages 44-47) with brushes, rags, plastic, or anything you like. When the effect is achieved, the glaze is allowed to dry. The paint effect will last as long as ordinary paints.

Glaze is available in oil- or water-based forms; the oil-based glaze has more luster and depth. When using glaze, take care to complete an entire section in one rapid session as, if the glaze begins to dry at the edges, you will see a significant "watermark" where the overlaps are. Stop in corners only, having brought the glazed section to a neat finish.

ENAMEL AND CRAFT PAINTS

These paints are sold in small quantities and are useful for small jobs, detailing, and murals. Their colors are very intense. Most enamels do not need to be protected with varnish and will keep their color for years. Craft paints, on the other hand, may be water based and might resist a surface that has been prepared in oils. Always buy the best craft paint you can afford. The color in cheap craft paint can fade rapidly.

ARTIST'S OIL CRAYONS

These crayons are just like children's wax crayons except that they are oil based. They can be used for touch-up jobs and for drawing fine lines where a paintbrush may be too bold, heavy, or difficult to handle. An oil crayon can be sharpened to a point just like a pencil, and the color can also be thinned or smudged with the aid of mineral spirits.

PURE PIGMENT

Sold in powder form by art supply stores, pure pigment is the base of all the traditional colors on an artist's palette. The color of pure pigment is the most intense available, and it can be mixed into either oil- or water-based products. It is expensive, but you only need a small amount as you will not use that much at a time.

LINSEED OIL

Linseed oil can be used to make your own transparent paints by mixing with artist's oil paints or pure pigments, a dash of mineral spirits and, very importantly, a few drops of driers. Use refined or boiled linseed oil to minimize the yellowing effect. Linseed oil does not dry without chemical help from driers.

DRIERS

These chemical additives can be added to oil paints to speed up the drying time. Be careful not to add too much; one teaspoon is sufficient for 32 fl oz (1 liter) of oil-based paint. Any more than this may affect the shine of the paint and make it appear powdery. Driers are an essential part of any painter's kit.

WHITING

A white powder, made from chalk, that can be added to homemade linseed oil paint to make it less transparent. Mix the oil into the powder a little at a time to avoid lumps, rather than putting powder into the paint. Whiting can also be used to make ready-made paints go further, but will have a slight whitening effect. Thin with turpentine, mineral spirits, or water, depending on the medium of your paint.

Troubleshooting

THE COLOR IS WRONG

If you are not happy with the color you have applied, you could repaint the room. Or if the color you have applied is fairly pale or light, consider glazing over it using a simple paint technique such as colorwashing or ragging. Your base color will be toned down by doing this but will still glow through the transparent glaze.

If the color looks too dark, you could try sponging one or two lighter colors on top. Your base color will show through but the whole effect will become lighter and mottled. If you are using two or more colors for sponging, use the lightest color last.

THE SHEEN IS WRONG

If the paint you have used either does not have as much shine as you would like or is too shiny, there is a solution.

Buy some latex glaze with a gloss, eggshell, or flat finish, whichever is required, and apply a single coat of this on the dry paint surface. Latex glaze looks like milk when wet but dries clear.

THE PAINT IS WAXY

Careful preparation can often keep oil-based paint from drying or make it dry with a waxy feel. If you are painting on a wooden surface you must first prime the surface. Primers provide not only a smooth surface on which to paint but also a base on which the top color will dry and cure fully. If you have overlooked priming the surface, wash the troubled paint away with plenty of mineral spirits and steel wool and start on a primed surface.

If the paint is drying very slowly with a waxy feel to it then you have probably applied the coats too thickly. The surface of the paint is beginning to dry and cure and is sealing in the moisture underneath it. If you can, let the paint alone for a week and see if it dries. If the paint does not dry, scrape it off, wash the wood with mineral spirits and steel wool, and start again.

THE PRIMER IS NOT DRYING

This is a rare problem and is usually caused by the primer having been applied too thickly. Primer should be thin and soak into the new wood when applied, providing a smooth and even surface on which to apply the top color. If the room in which you are working is damp you may also encounter problems with drying. Try heating the room with a dry heat and see if the primer dries. If it still does not dry, scrape off the offending primer and begin again.

PAINT HAS BEEN SPILLED

Every painter's nightmare is to spill paint on the carpet. If the spill is small, let it dry without touching it at all. It can then be removed from the carpet pile with sandpaper. Water-based paint spills can be removed immediately by washing the area with plenty of water and blotting with clean rags. Larger oil-based spills will have to be washed with mineral spirits and then with soapy water. Before washing out a spill, remove all the paint you can by scraping from the outside of the spill to the center.

NOT ENOUGH PAINT

If you notice the potential disaster of your paint running out in good time you can stretch your paint by diluting it a little with the appropriate thinner and by making sure that you use every drop of the paint in which you have soaked your rollers and brushes rather than washing it away into the sink. Sometimes you can buy a small tester pot of latex paint to help with that last small area. If you are working with a color that you mixed yourself, and that cannot be repeated, then one wall or section of your room will have to be painted in a harmonizing shade or color.

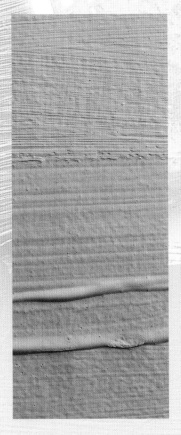

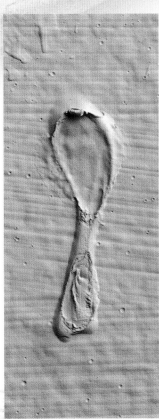

SAGGING

The paint has been applied too thickly or each coat has not been allowed to dry fully before the next was applied. To deal with sagging paint you must first allow it to dry fully and then rub the offending areas down with wet-and-dry sandpaper (use it wet for best results) until it is perfectly smooth. Now paint the rubbed-down parts again using the same number of coats you used on the whole area.

POOR FLOW LEVEL

The effect pictured above is caused by poor flow level, which means that the paint is resisting the surface on which it is being applied. It usually occurs when water-based paint, such as latex, is being applied on oil-based paint. For large areas you will be forced to buy new paint in oil-based form. For smaller areas, try washing the surface with detergent and a light scouring pad to remove any grease that may be sitting on the surface. If the paint still resists, you will have to resort to using oil-based paint.

CRACKING

Cracking is caused when paint or varnish is applied over a base layer of paint or varnish of different elasticity before it has been given long enough to cure (which can take up to a month). For example, two separate brands of varnish may react with each other and form cracks. To deal with cracking you must allow the surface to dry fully and then rub it down to make it ready for repainting. You could, however, consider leaving the cracking visible. It is a very popular aging technique, and many people seek this particular decorative effect.

DRIPS

Drips or "nibs" in the dried paint surface are usually simply oversights. Rub the dried drip away with fine sandpaper and repaint the area. On high-gloss finishes you may need to apply a final coat over the entire area to disguise the patch where you rubbed away a drip.

21

Product	Quality	Thinners and brush cleaning	Use for	Apply with
Primer	Preparation for bare wood. Keeps wood from swelling	Turpentine or water (check the can)	Bare wood	Brush or small roller
Undercoat	Flat finish, thin surface preparation and sealer	Water or turpentine (check the can)	Walls, woodwork	Brush
Latex flat	No shine, general-purpose coverage	Water	Walls, new plaster	Large brush or roller
Latex satin	Satin sheen, general-purpose coverage	Water	Walls, murals, base for glaze work. Not for new plaster	Large brush or roller
Eggshell	Satin sheen, general-purpose coverage	Mineral spirits or turpentine	Walls, woodwork, and metal	Large brush or roller
Gloss	High shine, durable	Turpentine or water (check the can)	Woodwork, doors	Good-quality brush
Wood stain	Color without varnish for bare wood	Water or mineral spirits	Bare or unvarnished wood	Lint-free cloth or brush
Varnish—polyurethane	Oil-based wood and paintwork protection. Choice of shine	Mineral spirits or turpentine	Wood and to protect paintwork	Good-quality brush
Varnish—water-based	Fast-drying protection for wood and paintwork. Choice of sheen. Nonyellowing	Water	Wood and to protect paintwork	Brush or roller

Number of coats	Washable?	Area per quart (liters) in square yards (meters)	Notes	Drying time pre recoating	Drying time final coat	Undercoat
1	N/A	13 yards (12 meters)	Thin to a watery consistency. Rub down with sandpaper when dry	2–4 hours	N/A	No
1	N/A	13 yards (12 meters)	Stir well. Rub down with sandpaper when dry	Oil based - 8 hours. Water based - 2 hours	N/A	N/A
2	No	11 yards (10 meters)	Do not stir and avoid frost	1–2 hours	8 hours	No, but dilute first coat for raw wood
2	Yes, soapy water. Do not scrub	11 yards (10 meters)	Dark colors require 3 or more coats	1–2 hours	8 hours	Latex flat
2	Yes, household cleaners. Avoid ammonia	16 yards (15 meters)	Stir well before and during use	8 hours	24 hours	Primer or commercial undercoat
2	Yes, household cleaners. Avoid ammonia	13 yards (12 meters)	Slow to apply—use good-quality bristle brush. Oil based is more long wearing	4–8 hours	24 hours	Primer
1 or 2	No	8 yards (8 meters)	Apply generously with brush or cloth. When dry, wipe off excess with dry cloth. Stainers do not protect wood; always wax or varnish when dry	1–3 hours	1–3 hours	No
Up to 8	Yes, soapy water	11 yards (10 meters)	Use thinned and apply several coats for the greatest luster. May yellow as coats build up	4 hours	24 hours	No
Up to 8	Yes, but do not scrub	11 yards (10 meters)	Difficult to apply as evenly as polyurethane varnishes. Not as durable but quick drying and crystal clear. Do not use on oil-based paints	1 hour	8 hours	No

23

Product	Quality	Thinners and brush cleaning	Use for	Apply with
Wax	Protection and shine for wood	N/A	Bare or stained wood	Lint-free cloth
Oil-based glaze	Transparent	Mineral spirits or turpentine	Mix with artist's oils to make colored glaze for various paint finishes	Brush or roller
Craft paint	Intense colors for detailing and small areas	Various	Small craft projects	Soft brush
Artist's oil crayons and pastels	Intense, pure colors in stick form	Oil or turpentine	Detailing and drawing on walls, furniture, or paper	N/A
Pigment	Intense colors	Water	Make homemade paints for color-washing	Brush or roller
Car spray paint	Low or high sheen, durable, wide color range	Cellulose thinners	Stencils and basic coverage	Spray from the can
Glass paint	Transparent or matte	Acetone	Painting glass of all kinds. Transparent detail work	Soft artist's brush
Blackboard paint	Matte black, very opaque	Denatured alcohol	Interior matte finishes, blackboards	Brush
PVA glue	General-purpose sealer	Water	Walls or woodwork to seal or stick	Brush

Number of coats	Washable?	Area per quart (liter) in square yards (meters)	Notes	Drying time pre recoating	Drying time final coat	Undercoat
3	Yes, with more wax or soapy water	8 yards (8 meters)	Apply just like shoe polish, buff with a soft cloth between coats. Pure beeswax best for new wood; rewax often	3 hours	N/A	Wood stain (optional)
1 or 2	No	Depends on consistency	Good workability for ½ hour. Cheap way to extend colour	6 hours	N/A	Oil-based eggshell base
1 or 2	Yes, do not scrub	N/A	Better quality than poster paints. Widely available in small quantities	½ hour	N/A	N/A
N/A	No	N/A	Allow to dry for 3 weeks or more before varnishing	N/A	N/A	N/A
1	Yes	N/A	Can be mixed with oil- or water-based products	N/A	N/A	N/A
1 or 2	Yes	N/A	Extremely long wearing; wear a mask when spraying	1 hour	10 hours	Spray undercoat
1	Yes, do not scrub; check label	N/A	Brushstrokes always show up; beautiful vivid color selection	1 hour	4 hours	No
1 or 2	Yes, water only	11 yards (10 meters)	Fast drying, easy to repair and patch up	1 hour	4 hours	No
1	Yes, soapy water	13 yards (12 meters)	Dilute 1:1 with water. Apply with brush	1–2 hours	N/A	No

25

MAKEOVER PROJECT

The Pastel Tones

This living room, which has been painted like a harlequin's jacket in four different colors, will challenge your ideas about color harmony, opposite colors, and shade. The secret here is tone; all the colors used in this room are of the same intensity. The only rebel in the tonality is the deeper shade of purple featured in the rabbeted shelves.

The inspiration for the decorating scheme for this room came from various sources. The mixed pastel colors are reminiscent of old-fashioned

PROJECTS FROM THIS
MAKEOVER SHOW YOU

- HOW TO PREPARE AN
  OIL-BASED SURFACE

- HOW TO CHOOSE AND
  USE OPPOSITE COLORS

- HOW TO PAINT A ROOM
  WITHOUT MASKING OFF

- HOW TO LAY A TONGUE
  AND GROOVE FLOOR

- HOW TO MAKE A BOX
  DISPLAY FRAME

sugared almonds while the powdery finish is rather like pastel chalks. Look at the colors on a paint chart for ideas of colors to use.

Using pastel tones makes a room feel more spacious. The mixed colors work together to create an atmosphere of calm and serenity; using yellow for the ceiling against the blue of the side walls makes the ceiling feel lower.

The paint used has a flat finish, producing a somewhat powdery effect. To achieve the finish and to create the depth of color required will take several coats. Paint the walls first, then the baseboards; there is no need to mask these as you can cover up rough edges later.

PREPARING AN OIL-BASED SURFACE

If your walls have previously been painted with oil-based paints, you will need to prepare them prior to painting with water-based latex paint. To do this wash down the surface with heavy-duty cleaner or a solution of detergent and water, using a scouring pad. This will provide a "key" for the water-based paint to adhere to. Even after this treatment, your first coat of paint may resist a little but the second coat will fill any gaps. You will need at least three coats of latex paint to cover an oil-based surface. Allow each coat to dry thoroughly before applying the next one.

FINDING COMPLEMENTARY AND OPPOSITE COLORS

If you cannot decide on the combination of colors to use in your room, you need first to decide which colors go well together without clashing. Using the color wheel is a simple way of discovering complementary and contrasting colors. To find an opposite color quickly and easily, simply stare hard at the first color for a minute or so and then transfer your gaze to a white surface. Wait about 15 seconds and the opposite color will reveal itself—it's just like looking at a yellow sun and then seeing a purple dot in your vision, only safer.

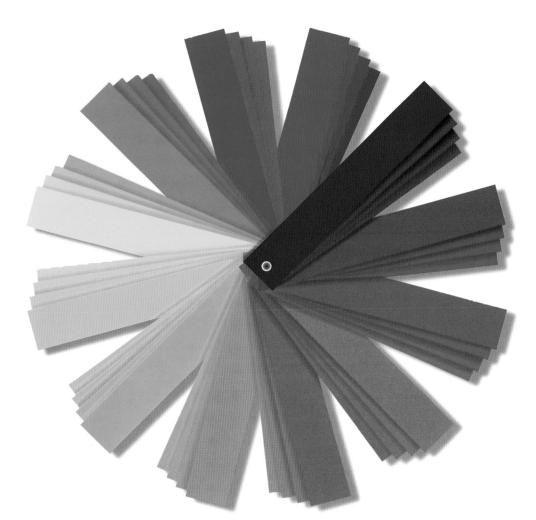

THE COLOR WHEEL

The color wheel illustrates the basics of color theory. Colors directly opposite are negatives of each other and therefore work well to create contrast. Colors found in the same quarter are known as "analogous" and harmonize as color families. Colors exactly one third apart on the wheel are called triadic and are a safe way of choosing a rainbow of colors without any clashing.

With red, for example, you can use green for contrast and more dramatic effect or orange and orange/red for relaxing harmony. The rainbow effect could be created safely by using red, yellow, and violet.

Painting a room

This method of painting a room in different pastel shades ensures a quick transformation without the necessity of masking off each section as you work. After you have had some practice using this cutting-in technique on the first wall, the rest will be easy. You will be able to paint a room like this one wall at a time, leaving several days in between each wall without the end result looking messy.

1 Beginning at the corner of a room, use a small paintbrush to paint the edge of one wall pale blue. Don't worry about paint going over the corner on to the second wall. This will be painted over later in a different color.

2 Apply purple paint to the edge of the adjoining wall with a small paintbrush or varnishing brush. To achieve a neat edge, push the tips of the bristles into the right angle of the two walls, as shown. This is very easy and takes only a little practice.

3 Finish painting both walls using a paint roller and plenty of paint. Coat the paint roller in paint, then roll it over the wall to cover the surface. You will need three coats on each wall, allowing the paint to dry for one or two hours between each coat.

4 To paint clean sharp edges on rabbeted areas, such as the shelves in this room, apply the paint with a brush to within a few inches (centimeters) of the edge. Then paint up to the edges by pulling a loaded brush gently out of the rabbet. Work slowly to avoid flicking paint everywhere.

EXPERT TIPS
- *If your paint roller is not producing a smooth finish, this usually means that the pile on your roller is too long. Switch to a shorter pile or use a paintbrush, or apply the paint more thickly so that it "settles" before it begins to dry. Watch out for runs when applying paint thickly.*

- *Do not apply oil-based paints thickly as they may not dry properly, resulting in a waxy skin on top and soft paint underneath.*

31

hardboard squares,
¾in (3mm) thick

annular nails, ¾in (2cm)
long

hammer

tongue and groove strips

tape measure

1½in (4cm) brads

drill with small bit

nail set

old piece of wood

saw

Laying tongue and groove flooring

The floor featured in this book is made from "tongue and groove" pine wood. The long strips of wood fit together like the pieces of a jigsaw puzzle and the fixings are concealed. Solid wood strips are sold in two ways—laminated and raw. The wood used here is raw. If you use this type of wood, a ½in (12mm) gap must be left on all sides to allow for expansion. Without the gap, an untreated floor will eventually buckle and split. In this room the strips were thin enough to slot under the baseboard and expansion will take place out of sight. You may need to fill a gap with strips of cork or wood molding. Laminated wood strips are made from seasoned wood and are varnished or coated with a vinyl coating. They do not need gaps left between them.

Tongue and groove strips are sold in packages that clearly state the area they will cover. To calculate the approximate amount of flooring you will need, multiply the width of the room by its length, then divide this figure by the area quoted on the packages of wood strips. Round the answer up to the next whole number to give the amount of packages to buy. Always buy the wood in advance, unwrap it, and leave it in the room for which it is intended for two days. This allows the wood to "acclimatize" and reduces the expansion that occurs after laying.

1 If your floorboards are in good condition, you may omit this step and proceed to step 2. If not, you will need to cover them in thin hardboard. Lay the hardboard over the floorboards with the rough side facing up, and nail it into place at regular intervals, working in a pyramid shape to avoid bulging. The nail heads should sink into the hardboard so that no bumps are visible in the final flooring.

2 Lay the first strip of tongue and groove at right angles to the floorboards and at the edge of the room with the groove edge facing, or just under, the baseboard. Attach the strip to the floor with brads at every 10in (25cm); drill a small pilot hole before hammering in the pin, to avoid splitting the wood.

3 Once the nail is hammered in halfway, hold a nail set over the head of the brad, and continue to hammer until the brad is securely fixed. Using a nail set avoids damaging the wood strips with your hammer.

4 Work along the width of the room before starting on the second row with the leftover piece from the first row. Join the groove from the second row on to the tongue from the first, tapping to ensure a tight fit. Use a piece of wood to protect the tongue and groove.

EXPERT TIPS

• *If you have a concrete floor rather than floorboards, you will not be able to attach tongue and groove using nails. Instead, glue each strip of wood into place using a good-quality contact adhesive.*

• *It is important to hammer the nails into the hardboard in the particular order shown below in order to avoid bulging:*

10 5 2 1 3 6 11
12 7 4 8 13
14 9 15
16

• *For a balanced effect, measure the width of the room carefully before you start. Calculate the number of strips of wood that will fit into the space. If, because of space, the last strip of wood to be positioned will be very narrow, saw a little off this first strip before attaching it.*

Making a box frame

Hanging in the shelves at the front of this room is a little box frame that is a simplified version of the framing technique very popular in homes at the moment. This frame was quickly and easily made from an old sturdy box. Cigar boxes are ideal for this purpose. Some come branded with the cigar make and are attractive left unpainted.

1 Discard the lid and sand the surface of the box to a smooth finish. Paint the frame with a coat of primer, then, when dry, add a coat of water-based paint, reserving some of the paint for finishing, and allow to dry.

2 Insert the item to be displayed in the box frame. Secure it in place with a few drops of contact adhesive. Allow the glue to dry.

3 Have a piece of thin glass cut to fit the top of the box, so that it can be placed on the box without falling in. Saw lengths of beading wood to fit around the top edges of the box frame. Use a miter box to make neat mitered corners. Paint the beading to match the box frame.

4 Lay the glass on the box frame. To secure it in place, glue the beading on to the frame using wood glue. Hold the beading in position with masking tape while the glue dries. Attach picture wire to the back of the box frame with hanging fittings to complete.

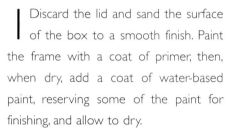

EXPERT TIPS

• *Sometimes these boxes come with sliding lids, in which case you could simply replace the lid with a piece of glass cut to size. If you prefer, you can use Perspex instead of glass; it is lighter, but is more likely to scratch.*

• *Mirror tiles placed in the bottom of the box can also work well if the back of the display item is attractive.*

MAKEOVER PROJECT

Versatile Yellow

Of all the colors in the spectrum, yellow is one of the most popular and widely used in homes. It brightens and warms, does not change the feeling of space, and can be used as a backdrop to many other tones and colors.

Yellow looks wonderful both in natural light and in artificial light; yet it also looks different in both. During daylight hours a yellow-painted room looks fresh and clear while in the evening light it takes on warm "oaty" tones, making it ideal for relaxing in. There are many shades of yellow

PROJECTS FROM THIS MAKEOVER SHOW YOU

- HOW TO PAINT A SMOOTH SURFACE

- HOW TO GET STRAIGHT LINES

- HOW TO DRAG A WALL

- HOW TO REHANG A DOOR

- HOW TO CREATE OTHER PAINT EFFECTS

you can base your decorating scheme on: the soft pale yellow of sponges, the sharp yellow of lemons, or the orangy yellow of sunsets.

This room is painted from floor to picture rail with a simple glaze technique called dragging. This effect is more formal and tidy than most other paint effects. Close inspection will reveal a thin stripe in the paintwork, no wider than a pinstripe, which subtly enhances the feeling of height in a room. A paler ceiling continues the effect and can really "raise the roof!"

The background for dragging must be smooth and painted with a brush, not a roller. Keep the glaze as thick as light cream.

PAINTING A SMOOTH SURFACE

The base coat for dragging must have a slight sheen to enable the glaze to slide around on top. Use either oil-based latex or water-based silk finish paints. To achieve a smooth finish, apply the paint generously with a brush in a criss-cross pattern on an area about a yard (meter) square at a time. Then gently feather the tip of your brush over the surface, finishing off with all brushstrokes in the same direction. Continue with the next square yard (meter) before the edges of the first have dried. This process is known as "laying off."

DRAWING GUIDELINES

It is difficult to create vertical lines around a room without eventually veering to the right or left with your brushwork. Once this has begun to happen it is very difficult to remedy and may continue to get worse as you work. You may not even realize it is happening until you reach a corner or stand back to look at your work. It is therefore advisable to mark the walls lightly with guidelines at intervals of 40in (1m) around the wall and then to follow these when dragging.

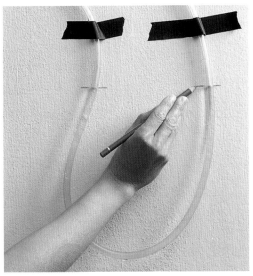

1 To draw vertical guidelines, hang a plumb line from the ceiling next to a wall (any weight suspended on a long piece of string can serve as a plumb line) using a pin or sticky pad. Lightly mark the true vertical on the wall with a ruler and a crayon in the color of your paint by running the crayon down the string. Repeat this at 40in (1m) intervals around the whole room before you begin to paint.

2 To draw horizontal guidelines, half-fill a 40in (1m) length of plastic tubing with water. Tape the two ends of the tubing to the wall so that the tube forms a "U" shape. Using a crayon, mark the water level at both ends of the tube; they should be at equal heights. Then draw a line between the two marks. Repeat at 40in (1m) intervals up the wall. Alternatively, you could use a carpenter's level.

Dragging a wall

Dragging is most effective when darker glazes are used over a paler background and when the shades used are noticeably different; for example, magnolia glaze dragged over a white base will not show at all. Likewise, white dragged over pink shows much less than pink dragged over white. The color of your top glaze (the dragging) will come across as the main color in the room. Here, fresh yellow is dragged over a white background making the room look yellow, even though the base color is pure white.

MATERIALS

32 fl oz (1 liter) oil-based scumble glaze

32 fl oz (1 liter) oil-based paint

approx 1 teacup mineral spirits

large all-purpose brush

dragging brush

1 To make the glaze, mix together the oil-based glaze and the oil-based paint, then add enough mineral spirits to thin the mixture to the consistency of evaporated milk. Using a large all-purpose brush, brush the glaze down the wall with vertical strokes. Apply the glaze evenly so that both edges are straight.

2 Immediately take a dragging brush and position it at the top of the wall so that the bristles and handle are vertical. Press the brush into the wet glaze so that it bends or flexes at the point where the bristles meet the handle and all of the bristles are in contact with the glaze. Holding this position, pull the brush all the way down the wall in one even stroke. The brush will produce fine stripes as it moves through the glaze. The pattern is formed at the point where the bristles meet the brush; the rest of the long hairs feather and soften the stripes.

• *Glaze that is too thick results in uneven strokes and stripes which do not run all the way from ceiling to floor; thin the glaze by adding a few splashes of mineral spirits at a time and stirring well. Do not be tempted to add a lot of thinners all at once—it is easy to overdilute glaze.*

• *If the glaze is not dark enough, and there is no contrast between the background color and the stripes, mix a teaspoon of artist's color into a small amount of the glaze, add this to the paint bucket, and stir well.*

3 For very high rooms, a good trick is to use a very soft household broom taped on the end of a long pole and work from the floor, stepping backward as you pull the broom down the wall.

MATERIALS

screwdriver

4in (10cm) butt hinges

utility knife

chisel

hammer

brass screws

wood filler

flat batten of wood

nails

fine-grit sandpaper

wooden wedges

Rehanging a door

Sometimes doors open the wrong way into a room, causing inconvenience to people entering and a waste of space in the room itself. This may be due to a previous use for the room or for aesthetic reasons. However, it is possible to rehang a door so that it opens the other way. This should always be done before decorating a room as it will involve some repainting. Rehanging a door is not technically demanding but it does take time and you may need some assistance as doors are extremely heavy. Allow a full afternoon in which to complete this task. Trying to rush it will only result in errors being made and the work having to be done again.

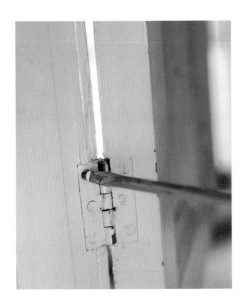

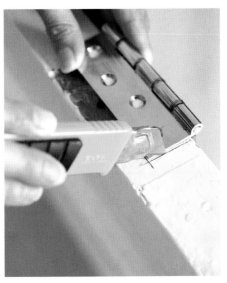

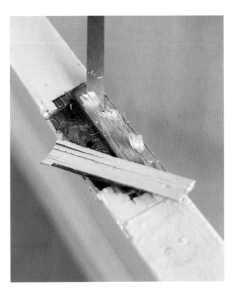

1 Remove the door and the hinges before buying the replacement hinges. It was decided to use larger butt hinges for this door but the same size would do just as well.

2 Using one of the new hinges as a guide, mark the position of the hinges carefully on the edge of the door, using a utility knife to score the outline. This cut will help when you chisel out the rabbets for the new hinges.

3 To allow the hinges to sit flush with the edge of the door and frame, chisel away the edge of the door marked in step 2 until the depth of the hole fits the hinge. Use a chisel and hammer with the beveled edge facing away from the center to ensure good straight cuts.

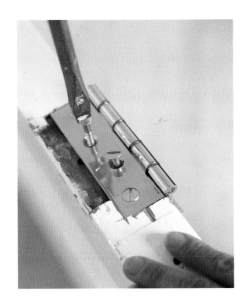

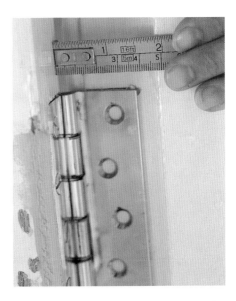

4 Screw the hinges securely into place using a flat screwdriver that fits the screw heads perfectly. A good-fitting screwdriver helps prevent slipping and scratching the new hinges.

5 Fill the old rabbet with wood filler. Loosely nail a batten of flat wood against the side of the door to provide a flat edge to fill against. Allow the filler to dry for several hours, then remove the batten and rub down the wood filler with fine-grit sandpaper.

6 Hold the door in position against the door frame and mark the position of the hinges on the frame as in step 2. Check that the door will close, then cut the new rabbets in the door frame and fill the old ones, as in steps 3, 4, and 5. Rehang the door, then change the latch from one side of the frame to the other.

Other paint effects

MATERIALS

FOR THE GLAZE

32 fl oz (1 liter) glaze

32 fl oz (1 liter) paint

paint bucket

all-purpose brush

mineral spirits or water

TOOLS FOR EFFECTS

stippling brush

cotton rag, 16in (40cm) square

plastic grocery bags

natural sea sponge

brown paper or newspaper

The dragging technique shown on page 40 is one of many paint effects that you can create using the same ingredients. Paint effects are created by moving a slippery, colored glaze around on a painted surface and then letting it dry. Different effects are created by varying the tool used to move the glaze. You can work with either water-based or oil-based products. Water-based glazes dry faster than oils but have less shine. Oil-based glazes may last longer, but beware of blues in oil, as they will go yellow behind pictures and in dark areas as time goes by. Exposing a yellowing patch to the light will eventually bring the color back.

Glaze techniques need to be carried out on a mid sheen base coat, such as latex satin or eggshell. Flat paint is not a suitable base for glazing over.

MIXING GLAZE

Mix together in a paint bucket equal quantities of glaze and paint in your chosen color; 32 fl oz (1 liter) of each will be sufficient for a room the size featured on page 36. Use oil-based (eggshell) paint with oil-based glaze, and latex satin paint with water-based glaze. Mix thoroughly with an all-purpose brush and dilute with mineral spirits or water, as appropriate, until the mixture is about the thickness of light cream. If you put some of this mixture on your hands, you will feel how it has a slippery feel, rather like cooking oil.

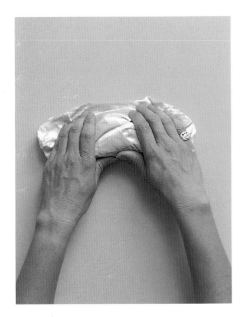

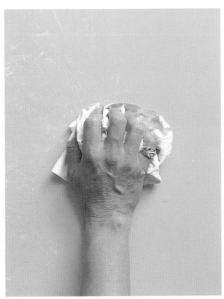

RAG ROLLING

Using an all-purpose brush, apply some glaze to the wall over an area about 40in (1m) square. To achieve a professional finish, stipple away all the brushstrokes by jabbing the surface of the wet glaze lightly with a large brush (see Stippling, page 47); using a stippling brush saves time and energy as it has a larger surface area than an all-purpose brush. Then crumple a cotton rag up in your hand. Keep all the messy edges and seams tucked away. Gently roll the rag up the wall, in any direction. The dry rag will lift the glaze away from the wall and produce a random pattern.

RAGGING

Ragging is a much subtler paint effect than rag rolling; it has more of a marbled look and is easy to do. Apply the glaze as before, working in areas about 40in (1m) square. Now gently dab a crumpled rag over the wet surface of the glaze. The more you dab, the flatter the final effect will be.

Cheesecloths will leave an imprint of the knitted surface of the cloth. Cotton sheeting is better if you are looking for a smoother ragging. Obviously, you must avoid lint in the cloths, so yellow dusting cloths cannot be used for ragging.

EXPERT TIPS

• *Always work fast from one corner of a room to the other without stopping and come to a neat finish. If the edges of your work begin to dry, a "watermark" will be evident at the overlap that is impossible to deal with unless you wash the whole wall and start again. There is no need to feel daunted by the threat of a watermark as all of these paint effects are very fast to do.*

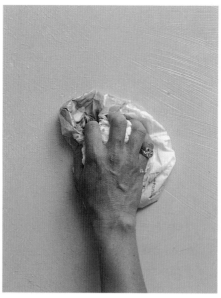

COLOR-WASHING

This paint effect is very simple to do. Dip a soft rag or piece of cheesecloth into the glaze and wring it out. Then wipe the wall with the wet rag in any direction you choose, in the same way you would if you were washing the walls with soap and water. The more you rub the paint into the wall, the more delicate the finish will be.

Work with a fairly thin glaze, like milk, in sections as large as you can safely reach to cover.

For an aged effect, apply a second coat in a curve around the top and bottom corners and around the ceiling join, rather like a misted picture frame. This second coat is fast to apply and gives a professional edge to the work.

BAGGING

This effect looks like old leather. A thicker glaze is best for bagging. Make up the glaze as on page 44 but without mineral spirits or water so that the glaze is the consistency of hair shampoo. Apply the glaze very thickly over an area about 40in (1m) square using an all-purpose brush; there is no need to remove the brushstrokes. Turn a plastic grocery bag inside out (to keep the printing ink from mixing with the paint) and crumple it up in your hand. Dab the crumpled bag all over the wet sticky glaze. Thicker bags make a more dramatic effect; try a few before deciding which one to use and make sure you have several of the same type to last you around the entire room.

SPONGING

One-color sponging tends to be overused by decorators; however, two-color sponging is very effective. You do not need a glaze for sponging; you can use any paint, directly from the can. Always use a natural sea sponge and try to find one that looks a bit hairy, with tiny spikes. Soften the sponge in water or mineral spirits before using it, then wring it out. Dip the sponge very lightly into a shallow tray of paint (the lid of the can will be fine). Dab the sponge lightly on to a piece of newspaper or cloth to remove the excess paint, then dab it very lightly all over the wall. Move your hand around into different positions as you go to avoid repeat marks. Use a tiny piece of sponge for tricky areas such as edges.

When you have covered the whole wall, repeat the process with the next color. Sponging the lightest color first works best; this produces an effect of shading. Always work lightly as heavy pressure will reveal the marks of the holes in the sponge rather than creating a soft speckled effect.

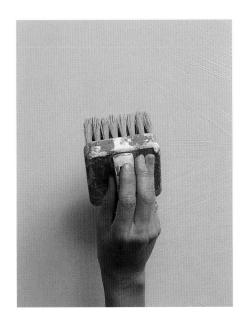

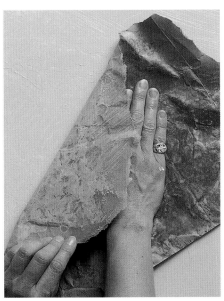

STIPPLING

Stippling is considered to be one of the most difficult paint effects to execute perfectly. However, the result is elegant and well worth doing. Work with a thick glaze as for bagging and apply the glaze in 40in (1m) square sections. Jab a stippling brush over the wet surface, revealing tiny pinprick marks, barely visible and just slightly textured. Concentrate on creating an even finish; stippling in its purest form should not look like clouds. Use the brush to move paint from darker patches by jabbing it into the patch and then on to a dry area of the wall. For a transparent effect, use oil-based glaze with just a touch of color.

FROTTAGE

This paint effect is messy, fast, and fun to do. Frottage produces a very random, mottled effect, rather like the look of old plaster. Working with a thin glaze and using more than one color can be effective, as can working with newspaper, which leaves touches of printing ink in the finished effect as a dirty tint. Experiment on a piece of white hardboard until you arrive at the effect you like.

Apply the glaze in 40in (1m) square areas with an all-purpose brush, then immediately press a piece of brown paper or newspaper on to the wet glaze. Pull it off right away to reveal the effect. The same piece of paper can be reused several times before it becomes too wet to absorb any more of the glaze.

EXPERT TIPS

• *If you are anxious to try several of the paint effects featured here before deciding which one to use in your room, paint trial samples on sections of white-faced hardboard (available from most home decorating stores).*

• *Alternatively, you can test the paint effect directly on the wall to be decorated, then depending on which type of glaze you are using, wash the trial area off quickly with water or mineral spirits before the glaze has a chance to dry.*

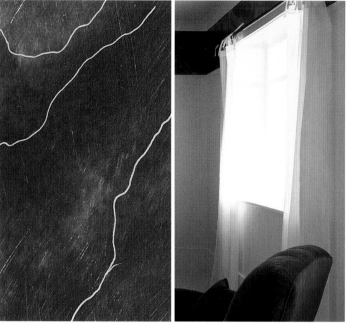

MAKEOVER PROJECT

Clean White

Pure, clean, crisp, fresh, cool, and unimposing: white is all of these. Unfortunately, it can also be described as boring, unimaginative, plain, and lackluster. This stunning room makes use of white, white, and more white, all brought to life with a single crafty accent color, ultramarine blue.

Contrary to popular opinion, white does not make a room look larger. Nor does it make a room look any lighter than, say, pale yellow or blue. White is cooling, however, and you must consider this if you are working in a cold room. Bear in

PROJECTS FROM THIS
MAKEOVER SHOW YOU

- HOW TO CHOOSE AN
  ACCENT COLOR

- HOW TO PAINT A DOOR

- HOW TO PAINT A
  MARBLED STRIP

- HOW TO DRY-BRUSH A
  WOODEN FLOOR

- HOW TO MAKE
  CURTAINS WITH TIES

mind also that evening lighting may yellow the overall effect unless you invest in low-voltage halogen or daylight-simulation bulbs.

The choice of ultramarine blue to accent the white keeps the room from seeming too cold. This strong color, which echoes the colors of an eggplant, adds a dramatic aspect.

The marbling technique seen around the top of the walls is simple to do and creates a softer effect than having plain painted cornices and chair rails. You can see the effect of horizontal stripes and observe how they draw your eyes along the walls, rather than up and down, thus reducing the impression of height.

CHOOSING AN ACCENT COLOR

There are no rules surrounding an accent color to go with a plain white room, and you are at liberty to select your favorite. Any deep or intense tone will stand out from the white, whereas paler shades will not stand out so much. Using black with white is not recommended, however; the contrast between these two colors is true negative and may play tricks on your eyes in bright daylight. Instead, use a shade close to black, such as Payne's gray, which is a dark blue gray, almost black, or a very deep brown, such as Vandyke brown.

These two colors just take the edge off a pure black and are a little softer to live with.

If you are superstitious, avoid scarlet and white; it would be better instead to go for an Indian red or alizarin crimson, both of which are deeper.

One way to choose an accent color is to consider the items you will be using in the room. One of these items will often dictate the color scheme to be used. If, however, you are starting from scratch, you can choose the color and then accessorize around it.

PAINTING A DOOR

Since doors are subject to a high degree of wear and tear, a strong and durable paint, such as eggshell or gloss, is recommended for them;

three coats will last for years. Paneled doors are very simple to paint section by section using the following method.

1 First paint the rabbets or panels of the door; apply the paint evenly in an up-and-down direction.

2 Then paint the center vertical of the door, leaving the horizontal bar unpainted for the moment.

3 Paint the horizontals of the door: along the top, middle, and bottom. Apply the paint in horizontal brushstrokes, leaving the sides of the door unpainted.

4 Finally, paint each side of the door from the top to the bottom with vertical brushstrokes. Follow the line of the rabbets for a clean finish. Allow to dry.

Painting a marbled strip

MATERIALS

2 teacups oil-based glaze

1 tbsp ultramarine blue
artist's oil

1 tbsp prussian blue
artist's oil

2 tsp driers

all-purpose paintbrush

badger softener (see
Brushes, page 90)

hog's hair softener (see
Brushes, page 90)

gold pen or fine artist's
brush and gold paint

In this simple method of creating the effect of marble, pure artist's colors are mixed with a thick, oily glaze and blended in diagonal strokes until most of the brushstrokes disappear.

Marbling is a technique that each individual does differently. So if you are working with someone, you should ideally work together on the same areas with one person applying the glaze and the other softening. Otherwise, if you both marble a separate section of a surface you will be able to see clearly the two different styles of work when they meet up in the middle.

When you are working above eye level, as on this marbled strip, you do not need to concentrate too much energy on blending and smoothing as the fine details will not be visible to the naked eye from the ground. Step down from your ladder now and then and observe your work from the real viewing points.

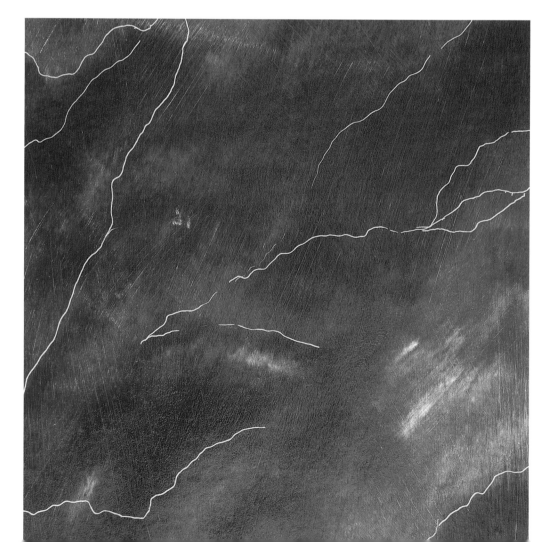

1 Mix two shades of blue glaze, using 1 cup of oil-based glaze and one of the artist's oils in each. Stir them both well and then add 1 teaspoon of driers to each glaze. Stipple or jab the glazes on to the cornice, using more of the prussian blue for a dark marble and more of the ultramarine blue if you are aiming for a brighter area. Bring the two colors right up against each other.

2 Working in sections about 1m (40in) square at a time, soften the wet glazes gently with a hog's hair softener. Stroke the wet glaze in a diagonal direction and gently blend the two shades of blue together. Most of the brushstrokes will still be visible at this point in the process.

3 Continue to brush the wet glaze in every direction to soften the brushstrokes using a badger softener. Wipe the brush clean regularly. If you are working at a height, you do not need to obliterate all the brushstrokes as they will not be seen from ground level.

4 When the marble background is dry, draw or paint some fine gold veins across the surface using a gold pen or a fine artist's brush and gold paint. The veins should filter into each other. Avoid making crosses or right angles as these would not occur naturally in marble.

EXPERT TIPS

• *If yellow patches occur in your white paint, there could be several causes. It might be damp coming through the walls, which must be dealt with, or it might be a result of the way in which the paint has been stored. Perhaps rust from an old can is getting into the paint. Let the paint dry thoroughly and then try covering the patch with a layer of new paint. If the stain still shows through you must seal the problem area with a curing paint, which is readily available from home decorating stores in cans or as a spray. Recoat the area with white paint only after the curing solution is fully dry.*

Dry-brushing a floor

MATERIALS

all-purpose brush

1 litre (32 fl oz) oil-based
paint in pale color

1 litre (32 fl oz) mineral
spirits

paint bucket

large all-purpose brush

When this tongue and groove flooring was first laid, it was protected with clear varnish, which allowed the natural beauty of the wood grain to shine through and reveal warm yellow or beechy tones. In this room it has been "dry-brushed" with a pale color. Dry-brushing is a fast and inexpensive alternative to liming (where white paste is pushed into the grain of the wood and then polished). The pale paint does not actually sit deep in the grain of the wood, but the effect is very similar to liming.

The paint will need to be protected from wear and tear after it has been applied; apply three thick coats of clear floor-quality varnish. After you have finished, store any remaining paint.

As with all floor treatments, the best way to do them is barefoot and just before you leave the room for several hours.

1 Using an all-purpose brush and a paint bucket, mix together oil-based paint in your selected color and mineral spirits. The paint mix should be the consistency of milk. If you are using a gel-type paint, you may need to add a little more mineral spirits to achieve this required consistency.

2 Brush some of the paint on a spare piece of wood, or in a corner of the floor that is not easy to see, to test it. It should be slightly transparent, enabling the grain of the wood to be clearly visible through the paint.

EXPERT TIPS
- *Always varnish a painted floor to protect the paint. You can apply varnish to a floor in quick, fairly sloppy strokes as it will settle to a flat surface as it dries. Look out for flying splashes of varnish that may land on an area where the varnish is already beginning to dry; brush any of these out immediately.*

3 Using a large all-purpose brush, dip the edge of the bristles into the paint mix and wipe off any excess on the edge of the paint bucket. Begin painting at the point furthest away from the door, and work along the planks one by one, brushing the paint lightly along the grain. Complete the planks one at a time but do not paint yourself into a corner.

4 The paint may soak into the wood in places so, from time to time, stand back from your work and look for any areas that do not have sufficient color in them. Go over these areas with more paint, feathering the edges of the patches with a zigzag movement of the brush so that the new paint blends into the paint you have already applied.

Curtains with ties

MATERIALS

tape measure

voile fabric

dressmaker's shears

iron

sewing machine

matching thread

These curtains are halfway between a traditional drape for keeping in the warmth and blocking out light, and a net curtain that prevents neighbours and any passersby from seeing into the room. They are made from a light voile, which allows a lot of light to pass through, and are secured to the pole with ties.

If you would like the curtains to hang flat against the window with just a few pleats when they are closed, then you will need fabric only one and a half times the width of the window. If you would like the closed curtains to have more volume, you will need two times the width of the window. This fabric was wide enough to use without having to make a seam. If you do need to join sections, oversew all raw edges with a zigzag stitch to avoid fraying.

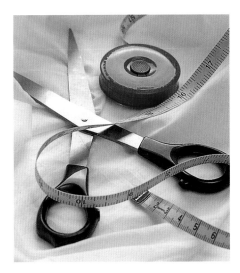

1 Measure the required length of the curtains and add 7½in (19cm) to this. Then measure the width of the window and multiply either by one and a half or by two, depending on the required volume. Add 6½in (16cm) to this measurement to make the total width. For two curtains, divide this measurement by two. Cut two drops of fabric of the required length and half the width.

2 Turn over ¾in (2cm), then another ¾in (2cm) at the side of the curtains, pin, and press. For the bottom hem, turn over ¾in (2cm), then 4in (10cm), pin, and press; for the top, fold over ¾in (2cm), then 2in (5cm), pin, and press.

3 Using matching thread in a sewing machine, stitch the side hems of the curtain. (A colored thread was used in the photographs so that it would be clearly visible.) Stitch the bottom hem in the same way.

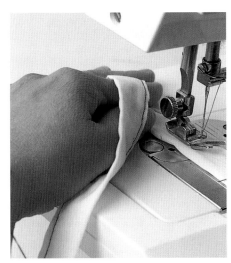

4 Cut rectangles of fabric, 14 × 3¼in (35 × 8cm) for the ties. You will need two ties for every 8in (20cm) of curtain. Fold each one in half lengthways, turn in the edges, press, and sew the sides together with straight stitch. Each finished tie should measure 13¼ × ¾in (33 × 2cm).

5 Hem the top of each curtain with a line of straight stitches, again using matching thread.

6 Attach the ties in pairs at 8in (20cm) intervals along the top of the curtain. Pin all the pairs of ties in place first in order to check that they fit well, with one pair right on each end. Adjust the spacing if necessary. Stitch each pair of ties in place securely.

MAKEOVER PROJECT

Neutral Brown

Capitalizing on sunshine, this room in its shades of

neutral brown is warm and welcoming; you could

easily relax here with the Sunday papers.

Deep shades of neutral brown need a sunny or

light room to work well. A quick look at the area

of shade next to the window in the photograph

will show you the graying effect shadow can have.

While most of the photographs in this book were

taken at the same time of day, notice how the

floor reflects the tones of the walls and in this case

has been toned down from a glowing cream to a

PROJECTS FROM THIS MAKEOVER SHOW YOU

- HOW TO MASK OFF AREAS

- HOW TO FILL SURFACE CRACKS AND HOLES

- HOW TO COLOR-WASH A WALL

- HOW TO UPHOLSTER A LOW BENCH

- HOW TO SHORTEN A VENETIAN BLIND

beech tone. Artificial light is not a problem with neutrals and browns; ordinary light bulbs have a slight yellow tone to them, which can enhance these colors.

The pinkish beige color above the picture rail was selected to echo the floor and furniture. Being paler than the color-washed walls it "lifts" the ceiling. The blue used on the ceiling is almost the opposite color to the beige above the picture rail and allows the introduction of blue accessories and fresher colors in the room. Careful selection of opposite colors for the area above the picture rail means that they counteract each other.

MASKING OFF AREAS

As color-washing requires large sweeping strokes, you will need to remove or carefully mask off any areas that are not to be painted. Loosen the screws on light switches, and plug sockets and carefully wrap the edges with masking tape. Use wide tape or newspaper to cover the remainder of the switch. For delicate areas, such as rails which are already painted, use a low-tack masking tape, which is not as sticky.

You can reduce the tackiness of tape by pressing a new piece of tape on to a carpet or a rag before use. After applying paint, remove the masking tape while the paint is still wet. If you allow it to dry you will undoubtedly pull away some of the paint from the wall with the tape. To mask off carpets, apply the masking tape and then press it hard on to the carpet. Tuck the edge right under the baseboard.

FILLING CRACKS AND HOLES

Many glazing techniques, such as color-washing, need a perfectly smooth surface to be effective. Any cracks or imperfections will hold a thicker layer of glaze and this will show up clearly as a deeper colored patch in the finished surface. However, do not panic; filling cracks is an easy process and it takes very little time to do.

EXPERT TIPS

• *Filler may sometimes bubble or drip out of large cracks and holes. In these cases you must first pack the hole tightly with newspaper or burlap and then fill over the Or apply the filler in layers, allowing each layer to dry thoroughly and sink down before applying the next.*

• *A flexible filler will take much longer to dry but will not crack again. It is worth using if your home is subject to traffic noise.*

1 Using a putty knife, press some filler into the crack, then carefully scrape away the excess. Always use flexible filler if possible; it will expand and contract with the crack and last longer than nonflexible types.

2 Allow the filler to dry and harden, then rub it down with medium-grit sandpaper to smooth the surface.

Color-washing a wall

MATERIALS

16 fl oz (500ml) oil-based paint

16 fl oz (500ml) glaze

approx 1 teacup mineral spirits

all-purpose brush

badger softener (see Brushes, page 90)

Color-washing is a term used so often to describe so many varied effects that it has almost become a generic term in the painting trade. It is actually a method for applying a thin glaze over the surface in such a way that the base color shows through a mottled surface. In this project the glaze is brushed on and spread out while it is still wet. The glaze, which is in liquid form, is added to the paint to give it a slippery texture so that the color will move about on the wall as you soften and spread it with the brush.

Color-washing must be carried out on top of a base coat of latex satin or eggshell rather than flat paint. The slight sheen of the base coat is very important for the softening to be effective.

1 To make the color-wash glaze, mix the oil-based paint with transparent glaze and stir well. Then add mineral spirits to thin the mixture until it is the consistency of light cream.

2 Using an all-purpose brush, apply the glaze over the wall, working quickly in large crisscross strokes, in sections about 40in (1m) square at a time. Leave some of the white base coat showing through between brushstrokes and overlap many of the brushstrokes.

3 Spread the glaze with the same brush, in crisscross directions, as far as it will easily go. This takes some physical energy but is very easy to carry out. Work fast and keep the edges of each section wet, overlapping each one as you go. Add more color if you wish.

4 Without allowing the glaze to dry, sweep a badger softener all over the wet crisscross marks in every direction. The soft bristles of the badger brush will obliterate most of the visible brush-strokes, yet leave behind the variations of shade caused by the overlaps.

EXPERT TIPS

• *Occasionally a thin glaze can become powdery when dry. This can be caused by a bad batch of ready-made paint but is usually caused by using an oil glaze that has not been stirred very thoroughly before use. To remedy a powdery finish, apply a single coat of latex glaze when the wall is fully dry. This is very thin and should be applied with a brush, not a roller, for best effect. It dries clear and serves as a washable and protective coat, a varnish, and a cure for powdery glaze work. Latex glaze is very fast to apply and dries in about an hour.*

• *When softening the glaze, make sure you do not stop unless you are at a corner, otherwise there will be a clear mark that will indicate the over-lapping sections and ruin the effect.*

MATERIALS

bench with cushion

furniture fabric

dressmaker's shears

sewing machine

matching thread

thumbtacks

stapler and ¼in (6mm) staples

muslin, optional

bradawl or skewer

Upholstering a bench

The blue bench featured in this room is upholstered in a thick-weave linen fabric. The effect can easily be emulated by re-covering an old bench. If you have never attempted upholstery before, don't worry, it is not as difficult as you think. The main point to remember is not to overtighten or overstretch the fabric as you pull it into place or the edges of the cushion pad will buckle. Use a thick fabric so that you can remove or reposition staples without tearing it.

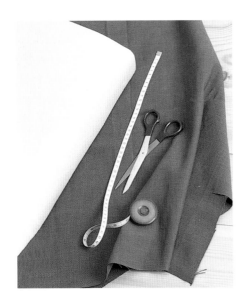

1 Remove the bench legs. Cut a piece of furniture fabric to fit all around the bench seat with a 2in (5cm) overlap on each side for the staples. In this case a rectangle was all that was required. Oversew the edges of the fabric using a sewing machine and machine thread to keep them from fraying; this is particularly important with coarse-weave fabrics, which tend to fray easily.

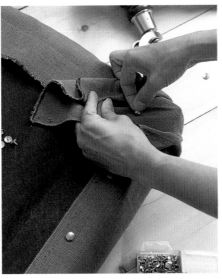

2 Stretch the fabric around the bench and hold it in place on the underside with thumbtacks. Fold the corners down neatly and secure these with tacks too.

3 While removing the thumbtacks one by one, stretch the fabric over the seat, securing on the underside with staples. Try to keep an even tension as you pull the fabric or the cushion pad will begin to undulate.

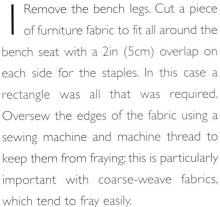

4 Hide any rough edges on the base with a piece of spare matching fabric or muslin. Staple this fabric to the base. You may need to trim the first piece of fabric at the corners to avoid bulging.

5 Once the upholstery is complete, reattach the legs of the bench. Use a bradawl or kitchen skewer to locate the holes, then screw the legs into place through the layers of fabric.

EXPERT TIPS

• *For those feeling more adventurous, fabric can be painted or embroidered for the bench. Commercially available fabric paints are durable through many washes but will not stand scrubbing, so you will have to remove the cover regularly for washing. For appliqué applications, the amount of stretch in the appliqué must be the same as in the main fabric or the stitches will tear and the fabric will not sit evenly when it is stretched on the bench.*

MATERIALS

tape measure

venetian blind

penknife or other knife

scissors

Shortening a venetian blind

Buying a venetian blind off the shelf is fast and often much less expensive than having one made to measure exactly. Unfortunately, however, they are often too long and the bundle of unused slats on the window sill not only looks unsightly but can be irritating as they knock things off and get in the way. Once you have learned this technique of shortening a blind it will prove invaluable!

• *If the blind is slanted when you hang it, you can adjust this using the main pull strings individually and then tying a knot in the bottom to keep them securely in position.*

• *The knot must, of course, be low enough to allow you to operate the blind but without it obstructing the actual mechanism.*

1 Measure the length of the window frame. Hold the venetian blind up against the window pane and open it fully. Count the number of spare slats that you will need to remove for the blind to fit perfectly.

2 Open the blind fully and lay it flat on a floor, making sure that all the cables and threads are straight and untwisted. Measure the blind, and check that you have calculated correctly the number of slats you need to remove.

3 Study the lower fastenings, making a mental note of how they are tied, as you will need to repeat this when reassembling the blind. Carefully open all of the fastenings using a penknife.

4 Remove the surplus slats and reassemble the lower fastenings before trimming anything from the cords and strings. The cables that support each individual slat must be cut apart before reattaching the bottom. Proceed carefully as the tiny threads that join these strings are essential to the spacing of the slats on a hanging blind.

MAKEOVER PROJECT

Classical Cream

Dispelling the myth that plain magnolia means anything without color, flavor, or imagination, this room uses the crisp cleanliness of magnolia tones and cream paints to produce a bright and classical atmosphere that was initially inspired by some of the work of the architect Robert Adam.

With a pale floor and walls, the eye is drawn to the deepest tones in the room; here these are the aging on the border and the coach lining (see page 72). A dark floor would also work well in this room and is worth considering if your room is

Stripping off old paint • Aging a wallpaper border • Gildin

PROJECTS FROM THIS MAKEOVER SHOW YOU

- HOW TO STRIP OLD PAINT

- HOW TO MIX AN AGING GLAZE

- HOW TO AGE A BORDER

- HOW TO MEASURE AND FIT A PICTURE RAIL

- HOW TO PAINT A FAUX STONE POT

- HOW TO GILD A CURTAIN POLE

cool. This would draw the eye down and create a balance against the border. If your room is already painted with cream or magnolia paints you will be able to begin with the border and careful accessorizing to create this look.

The floor in this room has been dry-brushed with off-white paint and varnished with three coats of polyurethane gloss (see page 54 for details on how to do this). Each coat of varnish takes about half an hour to apply and is allowed to dry overnight. Polyurethane varnish is very tough and long wearing. It will protect the paint finish for at least a year before it requires a further coat or two.

STRIPPING OLD PAINT

If your existing woodwork has been painted many times, you may have lost some of the definition in the carving. To strip old paint, and renew the shape of rails or carved details, apply a gel stripper to the painted surface by jabbing it on liberally with an old brush. Take care not to brush the stripper on as this neutralizes the chemicals. Once the gel has been jabbed on to the paint it will start to bubble. Remove the gel and old paint with a scraper; use an old toothbrush for intricate areas. If the paint does not come away easily, wait for a couple of minutes or apply another layer of gel stripper. When you have removed all the old paint, wash the wood with mineral spirits to neutralize fully any remaining gel stripper.

MIXING AN AGING GLAZE

It is possible to make a surface look old and timeworn without having to wait for this to occur by itself. In this room the border has been aged with a simple glaze technique, using a deeper and yellower tone than that used on the walls. Keeping to yellower, deeper tones not only provides harmony in the color scheme but actually produces the same effect as real aging. Most paints tend to yellow with age so white becomes yellow, pink becomes beige, and blue becomes more greenish. Mixing a drop of yellow ocher into the color you use will help you to find a natural aged tone.

1 Mix together a tablespoon each of yellow ocher and raw umber artist's oils with about half a cup of mineral spirits in a small pot. Stir the mixture thoroughly until all the lumps have dispersed. Add more mineral spirits if necessary until you have a thin, watery mix.

2 Pour the diluted oil paints into about 16 fl oz (500ml) of transparent, oil-based glaze and stir well. The glaze should be the same consistency as light cream.

71

Aging the border

MATERIALS

decorative border

latex satin paint

all-purpose brush

aging glaze

cloth

I tbsp yellow ocher
artist's oil

I tbsp raw umber
artist's oil

approx ½ teacup
mineral spirits

fine artist's brush

rag

The ornate border was ordered through a wallpaper supplier. It looks like flooring material and is very heavy to work with; it is actually made from linseed oil. Borders like this were traditionally used in stately homes and will last for 200 years or more. Allow the recommended paste to soak into the border for a couple of minutes before applying it; wipe away any excess glue with a damp rag. After pasting the strips of border, loop them into manageable sections to make it easier to carry them up the ladder. It doesn't matter if you get paste on to the good side of the border as it can easily be wiped away with a damp cloth. When applying the border to the wall, use the cornice as a guideline and butt the border up against it as you slide it into position.

Aging must be carried out on a surface that has a slight sheen to it. The border in this room was first painted with two coats of oil-based latex paint in pale cream.

EXPERT TIPS

• If the completed border looks too faint simply apply another coat of aging glaze. If your glaze work looks too heavy, however, dip a clean cloth in mineral spirits and wipe it over the surface, lifting off a little more of the glaze. You have about three hours to make this decision with an oil-based glaze, but only about half an hour if you have used a water-based one.

1 After painting the border with satin paint, in this case the same color as the ceiling, allow to dry. Then, using an all-purpose brush, apply the aging glaze (see page 71) in large crisscross strokes, working in sections of about 40in (1m) long. Make sure you push the glaze well into the moldings of the border with the bristles of the brush.

2 While the glaze is still wet, fold a cloth to form a pad and wipe this over the wet glaze. Most of the glaze will come away on the cloth, leaving behind only a trace of color on flat areas of the border and more defined staining in the crevices. Continue applying and wiping the glaze until you reach a corner. Any delay causes the glaze to dry and leave a mark where you start the next section.

3 For the coach lining, mix together the yellow ocher and raw umber artist's oils then dilute with mineral spirits to a watery consistency. Using a fine artist's brush apply the color to the carved lines on the picture rail, painting right into the grooves.

4 While the brown paint is still wet, wipe away any excess using a rag dampened with mineral spirits and wrapped around your finger or thumb. Run the rag along the edge of the groove to make clean straight lines. Use clean sections of the rag for each wipe.

Fitting a picture rail

tape measure

pencil

carpenter's level

picture rail molding

miter box

saw

wood filler

1in (25mm) brads

hammer

nail punch

The picture rail has recently become an aesthetic accessory rather than a functional part of room design and nowadays is used as a horizontal divider to add interest to the decor of a room. Some older homes still have their original picture rails, but if not they are easy to fit. You may use any design of carved molding to make your picture rail, and there is a wide variety available. This one is very functional, and the wood is sold as picture rail molding, which can easily accommodate a large picture-hanging hook.

1 Mark the position of the picture rail on the wall using a tape measure, pencil, and level. A picture rail is traditionally about 24in (60cm) below the top cornice, or the point at which the walls meet the ceiling. Measure from the ceiling at about 40in (1m) intervals and join up the marks to form the line of the picture rail. This picture rail was put up with the Robert Adam border in mind (see page 72), so the border was measured first and the rail then positioned to fit.

2 Measure the walls where you will be attaching the picture rail and cut lengths of picture rail molding to fit. To fit picture rail around a corner, use a miter box and saw to create mitered corners that join neatly. Any joins along the walls do not need to be mitered; the pieces of molding can just butt up against each other and be filled with wood filler.

3 Prepin the sections of picture rail at about 12in (30cm) intervals with brads. Hammer the pins just through the piece of picture rail so that it is already in position for you when you are balancing on a ladder.

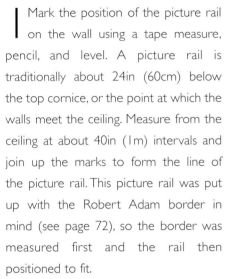

4 Following the pencil guidelines, place the picture rail on the wall. Beginning at the center of the rail and working outward, tack the half-fixed brads down into the wood, stopping before the hammer damages the rail.

5 Position a nail punch over each brad in turn and hammer the nail punch to finish driving each brad into the wood. This will keep the hammer from damaging the rail. Fill the tiny dents with a little wood filler.

EXPERT TIPS
• *A long carpenter's level will help you to plan the first guideline, but beware if your ceiling is not sea-level straight—and many are not. If your ceiling is not straight, you must measure down and follow the same line, as shown in step one here.*

Painting faux stone

The plant pot shown here has the look and feel of stone. But, if you pick it up, you will soon realize that it is feather light and has never seen a quarry or a stone mill. The pot is in fact a very inexpensive plastic urn bought from a garden center. This was then transformed with the aid of a few coats of cream and beige masonry paint which were dabbed and rubbed in with a brush and cloth.

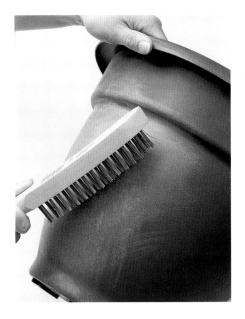

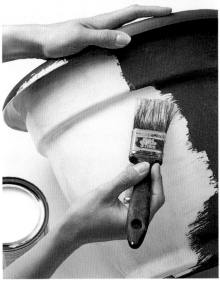

1 Rub the surface of a plastic pot with a firm wire brush or coarse-grit sandpaper until it is rough. This creates a "key" for paint to adhere to; paint would simply peel off a smooth plastic surface.

2 Using an all-purpose brush, prime the outside of the pot with a coat of white primer for glossy surfaces. Allow the paint to dry fully before moving on to the next step.

3 Paint the pot with at least two coats of cream masonry paint, allowing each coat to dry before applying the next; this paint has sand mixed into it at the manufacturing stage and it feels rough to the touch when dry. If desired, you can add extra sand to the paint before applying it for a rougher finish.

4 Paint around the moldings at the top and bottom of the pot with beige masonry paint to add shading. Dab the paint on roughly and rub it while wet with a cloth. Alternatively, you could rub rottenstone powder (gray pigment made from ground stone) into the cream masonry paint before it dries.

MATERIALS

curtain pole

burgundy latex paint

all-purpose paintbrushes

gold size

gold transfer leaf

gilder's brush

absorbent cotton

satin spray varnish

Gilding a curtain pole

Gilding a curtain pole is a small detail, one that many people will not notice in a room like this but it is in keeping with the aging on the decorative border, and it is the culmination of such small details that produce the final effect. The curtain pole shown above is gilded with tiny flakes of gold leaf, pressed on in handfuls and then rubbed smooth—a messy process. This project illustrates a smoother method of gilding that is easier for beginners.

Gilding on smooth surfaces is fairly easy to do and not expensive. It can still be rather messy, though, as small pieces of gold leaf tend to fly as you work. Gold transfer leaf, which is supplied attached to thin sheets of waxed paper, is easier to use than loose gold leaf and requires fewer of the expensive gilder's tools.

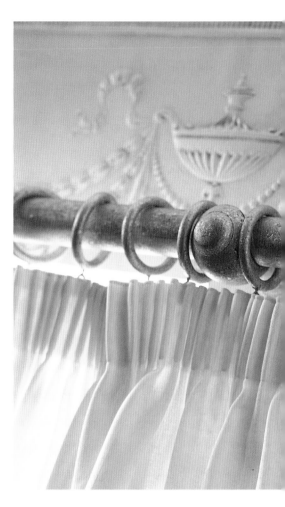

1 Paint the curtain pole with a coat of burgundy paint and allow to dry. This is a traditional-colored base for gold leaf. Then apply a coat of acrylic gold size (gilder's glue) all over the pole. Allow the size to dry until it is tacky to the touch; this may vary from 20 minutes to 24 hours depending on the size you use, so check the manufacturer's instructions.

2 Press pieces of gold transfer leaf on to the sticky size with the backing paper facing upward. Cover the whole area, leaving the backing paper in place. Allow the curtain pole to dry for an hour, then peel away the backing papers. Alternatively, to achieve the effect shown in the main picture, apply lavish quantities of loose gold leaf to the size, covering the pole completely. Allow to dry fully.

3 Using a gilder's brush or soft make-up brush, brush away the excess gold leaf to reveal the smooth gilded surface. If you have any gaps in the coverage, repeat steps 1 to 3 on these areas. Rub the curtain pole gently with absorbent cotton to smooth the surface.

4 Coat the pole with three layers of satin spray varnish; this will protect the surface and keep the curtain rings from wearing away the gold leaf. If your curtains are very heavy, apply four or five coats of varnish. Allow to dry for at least a day before hanging the curtains.

EXPERT TIPS
- *If the idea of working with delicate sheets of gold leaf is daunting, try putting the gold size on to the curtain pole, waiting for it to dry until tacky, and then brushing gold powder on to the size. While this is best done out of doors, you will find that gold powder sticks evenly; in fact, small items such as the curtain rings are easier to treat in this way. Varnish when dry.*

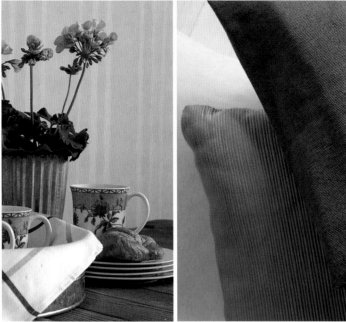

Bleached Blue

Sometimes the compromise forced upon you when deciding how to decorate a room is great; probably none greater than a room that serves adult purposes, such as relaxation in the evening, and the complete opposite during the day: kids! This room uses pale blues and fun stripes, all fully washable. The striking rug hides the ultimate in dual-purpose—a painted play mat to keep the children amused in their world of fantasies.

Blue is a cool color, particularly if the room faces away from the sun. Its opposite color is

PROJECTS FROM THIS
MAKEOVER SHOW YOU

- HOW TO CHOOSE SAFE
  PAINTS FOR CHILDREN

- HOW TO PAINT STRIPES
  WITH A ROLLER

- HOW TO MAKE A
  DISPOSABLE STENCIL

- HOW TO MAKE ZIPLESS
  PILLOWS

- HOW TO CORRODE A TIN
  BUCKET

yellow, which can be used to neutralize the effect. In a very shady room, blue can look gray and feel cold, so be careful when choosing shades of blue, and keep the color bright and cheery. The crisp blues used in this room were selected using shades from the same card in the home decorating store.

The striped effect is created using a foam roller and a ball of string, a simple and fast technique that takes half an hour to do. The play mat takes longer but is fun to paint. One advantage of painting for children is that they are less critical of your work than adults. You are not expected to turn out a masterpiece!

SAFE PAINTS FOR CHILDREN

Some paints may still contain toxic elements. Always check the can for full information and take note of any warnings on labels. Paints that advertise their "traditional" manufacture are likely candidates for a toxic ingredient, such as lead. Paints that have been developed for use in restoration, for historic houses and in association with the owners of heritage buildings, are even more likely to be unsuitable for use around children. It is therefore recommended to confine your paint choice to good all-around products that are sold in huge quantities each week and manufactured in the most basic fashion. The big paint manufacturers do not add any lead to their products, even though there may be a trace. They also use stainers that are considered safe and nontoxic.

PAINTING BASIC STRIPES

Basic stripes applied with a paint roller are fast to create; this room took only 20 minutes to stripe. Rollered stripes have soft blurred edges caused by the foam expanding and contracting as the pressure you exert changes. If you want tiny stripes, a small foam roller will be most suitable. However, a small roller will hold less paint and may not get you all the way down the wall in one sweep. Decide how to overlap with a newly loaded roller; using a paper or painted border to cover the overlap may be appropriate.

EXPERT TIPS

• *Do not worry if the striped pattern looks uneven where the roller runs out of paint. This is normal for stringed roller effects and is often incorporated into the design as intentional. If you prefer, you can overcome the fading by reversing the direction in which you apply the paint each time. For long stripes, wrap the roller less tightly with the string, so the sponge can still absorb plenty of paint for each stroke.*

• *If you are planning to paint a striped effect from floor to ceiling, reloading the roller and positioning it halfway up the wall may be necessary. In this case, make sure your roller is wrapped with bands, rather than in a spiral pattern with string, which will make it hard to reposition accurately. Start each stripe at a different level on the wall, thus avoiding a visible "reloading" area at about eye or knee level.*

1 Wrap string, ribbon, or rubber bands tightly around both ends of a paint roller, as shown here. The more sponge you can still see, the wider the stripes you will paint on the wall.

2 Using a paint tray with about ½in (1cm) depth of paint in the reservoir, dip the roller in the tray and load it evenly all around. Test the painted pattern on a piece of paper and practice painting an even stripe before starting.

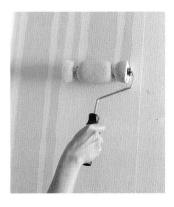

3 Attach a plumb line to the wall to act as a guideline. Apply the striped pattern on the wall, reloading the roller with paint after each stroke. When dry, brush a coat of water-based glaze over the top for a washable surface.

design for stencil

hard pencil

good-quality tracing paper

utility or craft knife

masking tape or spray mount

paintbrush or sponge

water-based paint

Making a disposable stencil

If you are not confident of your painting capabilities and are afraid to paint freehand, using a stencil will help you enormously. Most of the stenciled designs on this floor were painted only once, so a durable and long-lasting stencil was not required; disposable paper ones were made for the lettering and teddies.

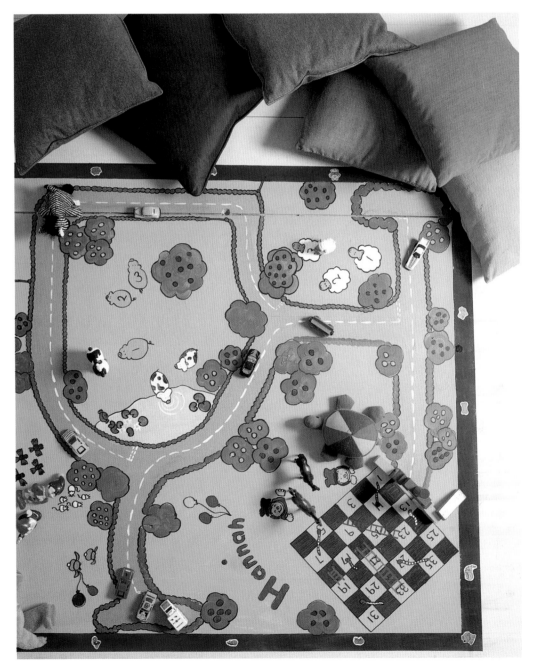

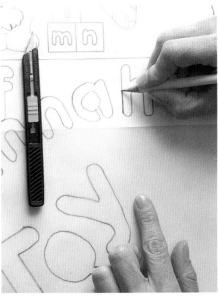

• *If paint seeps under the edges of the stencil, wipe it away with a cotton swab or piece of cloth dampened in water. Water-based paint can be removed after drying by gently scraping it away with a scouring pad.*

• *Alternatively, you may cover any bleeding by outlining the image by hand with a small artist's brush, possibly in a contrasting color.*

1 Find a design you would like to use for a stencil. Using a photocopier, enlarge it until it is the size you need. These images came from children's activity and coloring books.

2 Using a hard pencil, trace the enlarged design on to a sheet of good-quality tracing paper, readily available from art supply stores. Check that you have traced the whole design.

3 Using a scalpel or craft knife, cut out the design, leaving a gap between sections that will be painted in different colors, such as the sweaters and trousers on the teddies.

4 Position the stencil on the floor and secure with masking tape or spray mount. Then load a brush or sponge sparingly with water-based paint and carefully dab the color through the cut stencil. Lift away the stencil carefully as soon as you have applied the color and allow the design to dry.

MATERIALS

dressmaker's shears

fabric

tape measure

pillow form

steam iron

sewing machine

matching thread

3 buttons

pins

buttonholer

Making zipless pillows

If you do not like sewing, but want some new, inexpensive pillow covers for your living room, this project is ideal. These plain, square, zipless pillow covers are fast and simple to make and will add an instant splash of color to your decor.

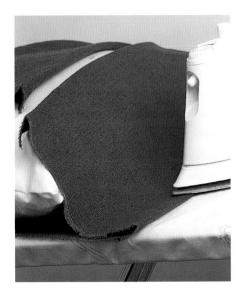

1 Cut a piece of fabric 2in (5cm) wider than the pillow form and two and a half times as long. Turn under the short edges of the fabric 1in (2.5cm) and press. Place the pillow form on top of the fabric and fold the fabric over the top, overlapping the edges. Press the side folds with a steam iron.

2 Using a sewing machine, oversew the fabric edges with zigzag stitch in a matching colored thread. This will keep the fabric edges from fraying when you wash the covers.

3 Make three buttonholes on one of the back flaps of the pillow cover. To do this, first measure the width of the buttons, then mark the position of the buttonholes with pins inserted ⅛in (3mm) wider apart than the width of the buttons. Stitch two rows of close zigzag stitch in between the pins, then longer zigzag stitches at each side. Slit the fabric between the two rows of stitching with a buttonholer, being careful not to cut the threads. Remove the pins.

4 Place the right sides of the fabric together, making sure that the flap with the buttonholes is positioned under the other flap, pin, then machine-stitch down the sides of the cover. Remove the pins then turn the cover the right side out through the back flap and press.

5 Sew the buttons on to the second back flap, making sure that they are in the right position for the buttonholes. Insert the pillow form and button up the cover to finish.

Corroding a tin bucket

MATERIALS

rubber gloves

goggles

face mask

tin or untreated metal
bucket

steel wool or wire brush

corroding chemical

old paintbrush

spray lacquer or varnish

The tin bucket in this room was purchased bright and shiny from a street vendor in South Africa. Tin items are widely available around the world. Some are available corroded, some will rust or corrode in time, and some, like this one, can be encouraged to age with a chemical process.

There is a variety of chemicals that can be used to corrode metal, some of which are noxious and must be treated with respect. Always test on a tiny area first as chemical reactions can be unpredictable. Remember always to work in a well-ventilated area or outdoors, and always have the correct neutralizing agent at the ready; this is normally a bucket of water or a hose. For protection, wear gloves, goggles, and a face mask when dealing with corroding chemicals.

1 Wearing rubber gloves, goggles, and a protective face mask, rub down the tin bucket with steel wool or a wire brush to remove any lacquer or finish applied in the factory.

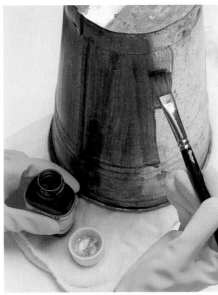

2 Paint or rub the corroding chemical on to the metal, taking care not to drip or splash on any areas not to be treated. Corroding metal just around the edges, where metal will age naturally, is very effective. The reaction should be immediate, but wait a while for it to finish.

3 Allow the corroded bucket to dry fully, when the chemicals may cause it to look a little dusty. Rub the bucket down again with a wire brush or steel wool, which will reveal some of the original shine.

4 Spray the bucket with a coat of clear spray lacquer or varnish to keep rust from forming, and allow to dry.

EXPERT TIP

• *Corroding chemicals can also be used on surfaces that have been gilded. However, be careful when using steel wool as this will not only remove the corrosion but the gold leaf as well. A craft store can supply or give you sources for the following chemicals:*

SODIUM HYDROXIDE—*This will corrode and blacken any untreated metals, but not stainless steel or highly polished metals.*

AMMONIUM CHLORIDE and COPPER SULFATE—*These are sold ready mixed as "instant rust," which creates real rust when applied to raw iron or steel. The rust develops for several days afterward.*

SODIUM SILICATE and IRON OXIDE—*These blacken any verdigris or rust finish as a second application. This is sold ready mixed as a blackening tint and is easy to use.*

CUPRA—*This green liquid corrodes any metal with copper in the alloy to create green verdigris.*

Brushes

NATURAL-BRISTLE BLENDER/ SOFTENER BRUSH

A necessary expense for any serious decorative artist, this brush is made from very soft, long bristles of pure badger hair. Use it to tickle away brushstrokes from wet glazes and to give an out-of-focus appearance. It is essential for marbling work and useful in creating a color-washed effect. Meticulous cleaning is important as badger brushes are expensive to replace. Condition them with hair conditioner regularly.

ARTIST'S BRUSHES

Usually made from hog's hair and very stiff, artist's brushes are invaluable for detail work and for mixing smaller quantities of paint. Cheap brushes are fine, unless you are using them for mural work, in which case better-quality brushes will give a more even brushstroke. The bristles of good-quality artist's brushes are slightly curved in toward the top of the brush, rather than being unnaturally straight.

FINE ARTIST'S BRUSHES

For detailing and fine mural work, a selection of medium-quality fine artist's brushes is important. Imitation sable or nylon work well and are less expensive than real sable or pony-hair brushes. Store them in a tube or brush wrap; do not store soft brushes in a pot with the bristles pointing downward as they will bend.

DUSTING BRUSH

This has endless uses, from dusting items before painting to dragging and color-washing. Natural bristle is more flexible and durable. Dusting brushes continue to perform well, even when they being to wear into a stump.

DRAGGING BRUSH

This is a special brush with extra-long flexible bristles for creating a fine, striped effect. If you have a choice of dragging brush, always select one with a comfortable handle.

FLOGGER

This brush has extremely long, floppy bristles that, when gently tapped into wet glaze, create the distinctive flecks seen in natural wood grains such as oak.

VARNISHING BRUSH

Not essential but a joy to work with, a varnishing brush looks just like a normal all-purpose brush until you turn it to the side and see that it is only about ¼in (5mm) thick. The bristles are very flexible, hold a lot of varnish or paint, and help to feather oil-based paints in particular so that a perfectly smooth paint surface is obtained with minimum effort. The brush with a dark green handle, shown in some of the step-by-step photographs earlier in this book, is a varnishing brush.

STIPPLING BRUSH

Use a stippling brush for removing brushstrokes and for creating a dotty, stippled paint effect. Most decorators use stippling brushes about 2in (5cm) square. Larger stipplers are faster to work with but become heavy as the hours pass. Stippling brushes are expensive and can be replaced in a pinch with a large paintbrush from which the loose bristles have been carefully picked out. If you use a paintbrush be sure to move it around as you work in order to avoid the imprint of the straight edges showing.

ALL-PURPOSE BRUSHES

A good selection of general all-purpose brushes is the starting point for any decorator. Buy the most expensive you can afford; cheap brushes will shed many hairs and not last long. When buying, press the bristles firmly to make sure there is no hole in the middle of the brisltes that has been filled with a wooden wedge. This will fill with paint and the brush will drip.

WALLPAPER PASTING BRUSH

Use this large brush for smoothing wallpaper into position on a wall. It is wide and comfortable to handle for long periods at a time.

RADIATOR BRUSH

This is a standard all-purpose brush attached to a long-angled handle; it is helpful for painting behind radiators and pipework.

SASH BRUSHES

Originally designed to help with the painting of complicated sash windows, sash brushes are available with pointed or rounded tips. They are perfect for edging and lining, and also for stippling paint on small areas or when control is required. With a little practice you will be able to apply paint in a perfectly straight line by using a sash brush. It may well become an essential part of your decorating kit and reduce your masking tape expenses.

CHOOSING BRUSHES

• *Good bristles have split ends, cheap nylon and bad bristles do not. It is easier to achieve a smooth finish with fine, soft bristles.*

• *Always use the narrowest brush you can bear as this will give you greater control and a longer period of time before a brush becomes too heavy.*

91

Tools

ROLLERS

Use long-piled rollers for textured finishes or uneven surfaces and short-piled rollers for a smooth finish. A foam roller is useful for a smooth finish with oil-based paints but may bubble or "orange peel." Work slowly with a well-loaded roller to avoid this. The small rollers sold for gloss paint are a useful addition to any painter's kit as they can be cleaned more easily than larger rollers.

SANDPAPER

Available in different grits, sandpaper is used for rubbing down and smoothing surfaces prior to painting, and for cleaning any drips of paint from a carpet.

ICE CUBE TRAY

Useful as a palette that holds a little sample of many colors at one time; it is easy to hold in one hand at the top of a ladder when painting detailing and murals.

MOHAIR PAIN APPLICATORS

These are wonderful speed painters, faster than a brush and smoother than a pile roller. Made from foam with a mohair painting surface, they are available in a wide range of sizes. These applicators are more economical with paint and much easier to wash than rollers. Work in every direction, adjusting the pressure from light to heavy as the applicator runs out of paint.

TACK CLOTHS

These are sold as disposable cloths on a roll, or separately packed. They are lightly impregnated with spirits and oils and are perfect for wiping away dust after sanding a wooden item prior to priming, painting, and varnishing it. The oils and spirits can also help with cleaning paintwork prior to painting, but heavy-duty cleaner should be used if you are going to use a water-based paint.

TOOLS FOR GLAZE WORK

Not all glaze finishes require expensive, special brushes. Plastic bags can be wadded up and used to create a leathery effect, corks can be jabbed in to the glaze for a fossil effect, and rags used to create a soft, mottled look. Experiment with anything that will not leave lint or fluff in the glaze—try plastic wrap or foil and even the side of your fist or your fingertips.

PAINT TRAYS

Not just for rolling paint, these are also useful for holding open cans of paint and for mixing small quantities of paint.

DISPOSABLE PAPER PALETTE

Use this for tiny quantities of several colors at one time. The tear-off sheets eliminate any cleaning at the end of the day. Very comfortable to hold for long periods.

PAINT BUCKETS

Sturdy and reliable containers for a can of paint or a glaze mixture. A bucket can be hung from the top of a ladder with a meat hook or the handle. Keep an empty bucket handy for putting wet brushes in. Plastic buckets need not be washed after use and can be reused after the paint has dried until eventually you throw them away. Steel buckets are more expensive and therefore require more care and cleaning.

MAULSTICK

This is a cane with a soft ball of chamois leather or cloth tied to the end. For high work that requires a very steady hand, hold the maulstick in your nonpainting hand, supporting the cane under your arm. Rest the ball on the wall. You can then rest your painting wrist on the stick and remain steady, even for minute details. You can make a maulstick by attaching a cut tennis ball to one end of a cane with a large square of chamois leather wrapped over the ball and tied securely to the cane.

Suppliers & Acknowledgments

Arc Prints
Wandsworth Bridge Road
London SW6
Tel: 0171-731 3933
Framed prints

Atlantis Arts
146 Brick Lane
London E1 6RU
Tel: 0171-377 8855
Artist's oils and brushes

C. Brewer & Sons Ltd.
327 Putney Bridge Road
Putney
London SW15 2PG
Tel: 0181-788 9335
Sundries and brushes

The Dormy House
Stirling Park
East Portway Industrial Estate
Andover
Hampshire SP10 3TZ
Tel: 01264 365808
Benches and other furniture.
Mail order only

ICI Paints
Wexham Road
Slough SL2 5DS
Tel: 01753 534 225
Paints

E. Ploton
273 Archway Road
London N6 5AA
Tel: 0181-348 2838
Gilding and artist's supplies

Thanks are due to the following companies who supplied props used in photography:

Colour Blue
9 Gilbert Road
London SE11 4LN
Tel: 0171-820 7700
Blue wooden bench seat and coffee table; call for a brochure

Peter Guild
84-92 College Street
Kempston
Bedford MK42 8LU
Tel: 01234 273372
Cream sofa and armchair and dark purple sofa and chair; call for a prochure

Mulberry Flowers
11 Croxted Road
West Dulwich
London SE21 8SZ
Tel: 0181-670 1022
Plants and flowers used throughout the book

Viaduct
1–10 Summer's Street
London EC1R 5BD
Tel: 0171-278 8456
Dining table and chairs

The publishers wish to thank the following photographers and organizations for their kind permission to reproduce the photographs in this book on the following pages:

p.6 top Christopher Drake/Country Homes & Interiors/Robert Harding; p.6 bottom James Merrell/Country Homes & Interiors/Robert Harding; p.7 top James Merrell/Country Homes & Interiors/Robert Harding; p.7 and p.10 Richard Waite/Arcaid; p.11 Petrina Tinslav/Belle/Arcaid; p.12 Jan Baldwin/Homes & Gardens/Robert Harding; p.13 Trevor Richards/Homes & Gardens/Robert Harding; p.14 James Merrell/Country Homes & Interiors/Robert Harding; p.15 James Merrell/Country Homes & Interiors/Robert Harding

Index

DEDICATION

For Robin Leach, with love

AUTHOR'S ACKNOWLEDGMENTS

Heartfelt thanks to those who work just as hard and then
don't see their names on the cover of this book: Dominic
Blackmore, photographer extraordinaire; Nel Lintern, stylist;
Albert Thompson, copainter; and Adrian Martindale, the
ultimate Man Friday. Also a debt of gratitude to Sara Colledge
and Anna Sanderson, tireless commissioning editors.

First published in North America
in 2001 by Betterway Books
an imprint of F&W Publications, Inc.
1507 Dana Avenue
Cincinnati, OH 45207
1-800/289-0963

Copyright © 1999 Murdoch Books (UK)

ISBN 1-55870-604-6

Editor: Heather Dewhurst
Designers: Siân Keogh and Martin Laurie at Axis Design
Photographer: Dominic Blackmore
Stylist: Nel Lintern
Series Concept & Art Direction: Marylouise Brammer
Commissioning Editor: Anna Sanderson
CEO & Publisher: Anne Wilson
International Sales Director: Mark Newman
Color separation by Bright Arts in Hong Kong
Printed in Singapore by Tien Wah Press